2020

As It Happened

2020
As It Happened

CALUM PATON AND NATHAN SHOESMITH

THE SPEAKER MEDIA LIMITED

The Speaker Media Limited.
Enterprise & Innovation Services ,Bowland Main,
Lancaster University,
Lancaster LA1 4YT.

First Printed in Great Britain by Amazon.

ISBN   9798707641893

CONTENTS

INTRODUCTION   1

JANUARY   5

FEBRUARY   19

MARCH   29

APRIL   45

MAY   59

JUNE   77

JULY   89

AUGUST   101

SEPTEMBER   115

OCTOBER   133

NOVEMBER   149

DECEMBER   167

CONCLUSION   181

SOURCE NOTES   185

ACKNOWLEDGEMENTS   199

ABOUT THE SPEAKER   201

ABOUT THE AUTHORS   203

INTRODUCTION

At one minute to midnight on the 31st of December 2019 we had hope for the year ahead. As we looked forward to the new decade, there was optimism that 2020 would be the year we finally closed the chapter on Brexit; the year that drastic action was taken on climate change; the year we fought to challenge structural injustices. A new decade would bring brand-new opportunities - that was the hope.

However, we also wished that 2020 would be a quieter year than the one before. In 2019 – a big year for U.S. politics – Donald Trump became only the third president in U.S. history to be impeached. After spontaneously tweeting an invitation to meet the North Korean leader, Trump also became the first sitting U.S. president to walk into North Korea. Whilst in the U.K., he stormed out of a NATO summit after other leaders appeared to gossip behind his back – Canadian prime minister Justin Trudeau seemingly mocked Trump's erratic behaviour.

In the United Kingdom, 2019 had seen Theresa May give a tearful resignation speech from the steps of Downing Street, with Boris Johnson winning the Conservative Party leadership election to replace her. In December, an early general election saw the triumph of the Conservatives with their largest majority since 1987; the resignations of Labour Leader Jeremy Corbyn and Jo Swinson as Liberal Democrat leader, with the latter losing her own seat in Parliament.

Above all this, Brexit dominated our lives and Britain's exit date was pushed back on multiple occasions and into 2020. 3 years since the EU Referendum in which Britons voted by 52% to leave the European Union, as people became tired of seemingly endless debates about Brexit, we hoped that 2020 might finally see Brexit knocked out of the headlines.

2020 delivered on that wish, however the new topic of discussion proved even less welcome.

Unbeknownst to the world, as the new decade got underway, 2020 was to be one of the most difficult years in modern history. Faced by a global health emergency, the world went into lockdown, with people having to stay at home, live online and distance themselves from loved ones like never before.

2020 was a year of losing so much, and tragically, so many. As over a million people lost their lives to the deadly coronavirus pandemic, families were left heartbroken; few were untouched by the tragedies of the year. Lives changed in 2020, many forever, and the events of 2020 will likely shape attitudes and perspectives long into the future.

The world was forced to change and adapt. Our economies suffered their worst declines in history, with millions losing their livelihoods and many struggling to get by.

The tragedy of the pandemic may have been the most significant event of the entire year, but even without the pandemic, 2020 proved to be precarious. It was a year in which a sitting president stood in the White House briefing room and told America not to count votes; a year where there was a real fear of another world war; and a year where governments collapsed in the wake of corruption scandals.

2020 proved the most unprecedented and tragic year in modern history.

However, it also proved a year of hope. The world appeared to finally step up and take the legacies of slavery and institutionalised racism seriously. It was a year where activism proved perhaps more successful than it has in decades, with the United Kingdom amongst the nations to commit to ambitious goals in an attempt to combat climate change.

There were also stories of personal triumph. Of people throughout the world stepping up to raise money for those in greater need, or of individuals going the extra mile to support elderly and vulnerable relatives, neighbours, friends, and even strangers.

TikTok and other social media platforms became a global community providing light relief to people throughout the world, and the rise of Zoom and other video platforms allowed us to see that no matter how far apart we are, the modern world still allows us to be together.

2020 proved the majesty of science and innovation, with scientists developing vaccines within months of the coronavirus first emerging. Tireless work by scientists and health and medical experts provided hope for a return to pre-pandemic normality.

Each year at The Speaker, we wrap up the year in one article looking back on the major events that have hit the headlines. Every year, something happens that will be remembered for bad or for good, but 2020 really did hit a different level. Given the extent and sheer volume of major events and change during the year, we felt one article simply wasn't enough.

Our solution? This book.

For all those that lived through it, 2020 will be a year that cannot be forgotten, however hard people try. With no definitive date for the end of the Coronavirus pandemic, it is highly likely that the impacts of events in 2020 will be felt for many years to come.

Whatever happens in the future, it seems 2020 will always have an important place in history.

In this book, we look back on how we told the stories during times of uncertainty, confusion and monumental change. Featuring adapting reporting and analysis from a year like no other, this is 2020, as it happened.

JANUARY

World War Three Fears | A Virus Emerges

3rd | Iran

One of Iran's top military commanders has been killed by U.S. forces, resulting in an unexpected escalation of tensions between Washington and Tehran.

Yesterday (2nd), the Department of Defense confirmed that Qasem Soleimani, who leads Iran's elite Quds force was killed in what the U.S. described as a 'defensive action'. The 62–year–old was killed at Baghdad Airport in Iraq by a U.S. airstrike which was ordered by U.S. President Donald Trump. The Department of Defense said in a statement;

> 'At the direction of the President, the U.S. military has taken decisive defensive action to protect U.S. personnel abroad by killing Qasem Soleimani, the head of the Iranian Revolutionary Guard Corps–Quds Force, a U.S.–designated Foreign Terrorist Organization'.

The U.K. government has urged all parties involved to de–escalate. Foreign Secretary Dominic Raab said the U.K. 'recognised the aggressive threat' General Soleimani posed but said 'further conflict is in none of our interests'. It remains unknown whether U.K. Prime Minister Boris Johnson was made aware of the strike before it happened.

According to reports by Politico, U.S. officials, including some members of the Trump administration were 'astonished' by the killing, with one official saying 'I can't believe it' and another saying 'We need to be prepared that we're now at war'.

Iran's Supreme Leader Ayatollah Ali Khamenei has vowed 'severe revenge' against the United States, and has called for three days of national mourning. He said, 'vengeance is in store for the criminals who stained their unclean hands with his blood and that of other martyrs in the incident last night'.

3rd | United States

U.S. President Donald Trump has warned that he has a list of '52 Iranian targets' which he would 'hit very fast and very hard' if Iran attacked the U.S. or U.S. citizens.

Iran has heavily criticised recent tweets by the U.S. President as being threats of war crimes. In particular, Iran's foreign minister Javad Zarif described threats by Mr Trump as breaches of international law.

In a tweet, Mr Trump said;

'Let this serve as a WARNING that if Iran strikes any Americans, or American assets, we have targeted 52 Iranian sites (representing the 52 American hostages taken by Iran many years ago), some at a very high level & important to Iran & the Iranian culture, and those targets, and Iran itself, WILL BE HIT VERY FAST AND VERY HARD'. – @realDonaldTrump

4th | Australia

Thousands have been evacuated, and many more have been left homeless as fires continue to rage through millions of hectares of Australian land.

Fires aren't uncommon in Australia; the country regularly experiences bushfires, with even the coldest regions having barbeque bans throughout the annual fire season. Yet, in late 2019 and early 2020, the fires have raged far worse than usual. Since September, more than 6.3 million hectares have been burned – only slightly smaller than the total area of Scotland.

The fires have so far claimed the lives of two dozen people and the houses of many thousands more. Some estimates have suggested that over a billion animals may have been killed in the fires to date, and some endangered species have potentially been driven to extinction.

A natural weather phenomenon known as the Indian Ocean Dipole (IOD) has led to a particularly dry spell across the country in the past few months. Put simply, the IOD is an imbalance in seawater temperatures between east and west.

As Australia's skies turn orange and thousands lose their homes, many have been asking whether the fires can be linked to climate change. Some Australian politicians and leaders have refused to answer questions on climate change, and many members of the public have accused the government of not doing enough to combat it. Prime Minister Scott Morrison has come under fire for taking a holiday during the height of the fires at the end of 2019, with his popularity at its lowest point since he took office last year.

Linking climate change to any specific incident is difficult, but it would certainly appear that climate change is contributing to the intensity of the fires.

The Australian summer sees the country's hottest months in December, January, and February. Since last June, fires have been raging and are still ongoing, with no clear end date in sight.

8th | United Kingdom

MPs in the House of Commons have given their final backing of Boris Johnson's Brexit Deal that is due to see the U.K. leave the E.U. on the 31st of January.

The Withdrawal Agreement Bill passed its third reading with a strong majority of 99. A total of 330 MPs voted in favour of the bill, while 231 voted against, the vote was almost entirely along partisan lines with only a handful of Labour MPs backing the government's deal.

Following the vote, Brexit Secretary Steve Barclay said the bill will deliver on the 'overwhelming mandate' given to the Conservative Party to take Britain out of the E.U. at the 2019 general election.

The Scottish National Party (SNP) and Liberal Democrats have continued to express their opposition to the bill.

The Withdrawal Agreement Bill will move to the House of Lords next week where it will face further scrutiny before it can become law.

The Withdrawal Agreement is just the first stage in implementing Brexit – once the U.K. has left the E.U., it will enter a transition period in which it will need to negotiate a future relationship with the bloc. The current deadline to do so is the end of December this year.

8th | United States

U.S. President Donald Trump has delivered a statement after Iran fired 22 ballistic missiles at two Iraqi bases housing U.S. and coalition troops.

There are not believed to have been any casualties from the attack, and only minor damage is understood to have impacted the bases. It is instead believed to have been more of a warning shot than an all–out attack.

Speaking in the White House's grand foyer, the President Trump began his statement by saying 'Iran will never be allowed to have a nuclear weapon as long as I am president'.

In what appeared to show the U.S. now pursuing a diplomatic approach to resolving the current crisis in Iran, President Trump did not announce any major response to the attack, except increased economic sanctions on Iran.

Speaking about General Soleimani, Mr Trump said he had been responsible for the 'absolute worst atrocities', including the killing of thousands of U.S. troops. He said that General Soleimani should have been terminated 'a long time ago' and said Iran must abandon its nuclear ambitions and support for terrorism.

The U.S. president also called on powers in Europe, Russia, and China to abandon the 2015 Iran nuclear deal and work together to agree on a new deal with Iran.

Ending his statement, Mr Trump said the U.S. is ready to 'embrace peace with all who seek it', adding 'God bless America'.

8th | Iran

A Ukrainian passenger plane has crashed shortly after taking off from the Imam Khomeini Airport in Tehran, Iran.

Ukraine International Airlines flight PS752 was travelling to Ukraine's capital Kyiv after taking off at 6.12 am local time. The plane, carrying 176 passengers and crew, sent its last signal two minutes after taking off. The crash is thought to have left no survivors.

One of the aircraft's black boxes has been found by rescue workers, according to Iranian media. Ukraine International Airlines has suspended flights to Tehran indefinitely and said that the plane involved in the crash had completed its last scheduled maintenance just two days earlier.

Ukrainian Foreign Minister Vadym Prystaiko has said that 82 of the victims were Iranians, 63 were Canadians, 11 were Ukrainians, and there were 10 Swedes, 4 Afghans, 3 Germans and 3 Britons on board, who are all thought to have died in the crash.

8th | United Kingdom

The Duke and Duchess of Sussex, Prince Harry and Meghan Markle, have announced on social media that they intend to step back from their positions as senior royals.

They have stated that they desire to be financially independent of the royal family and free of much of the media scrutiny of the couple; the British press have been accused of biased reporting and being vicious towards Meghan Markle, particularly when compared to the coverage of Prince William's wife, Kate Middleton.

The couple will split their time between the United Kingdom and the United States.

The decision – considered the second most important impending exit of January 2020, aside from Brexit – has spawned a mixed reaction on social media, with some praising their decision to be financially independent. Others consider the move to be either a publicity stunt or not news at all. Some have criticised the couple for recently spending large amounts of taxpayer's money on refurbishing their matrimonial home, Frogmore Cottage, just months before announcing their decision to leave.

8th | Venezuela

Venezuela has suffered from political unrest for several months, after a controversial presidential election which saw incumbent President Nicolas Maduro retain power in an election that was widely reported as fraudulent.

In the following months, many countries including neighbouring Argentina had recognised Juan Guaido, the opposition leader, as the rightful victor.

Today, the situation appears to have escalated. Just two days after Guaido was prevented from entering the parliament by the national guard – eventually climbing a fence and later being allowed in – protests on the streets have left countless injured.

Opponents of the opposition leader have said that now is the time to reconcile with Maduro and for a line to be drawn under the election, despite international observers still stating that the election was fraudulent.

Guaido has been supported in his efforts by a number of international leaders, with many claiming that the election result should be voided.

Maduro is backed by Russian President Vladimir Putin, and has been in power since the death of socialist ruler, Hugo Chavez, in 2013.

Recent years have been underlined by an economic crisis that has led to severe supply shortages and inflation, leaving millions in poverty.

9th | Iran

According to U.K. Prime Minister Boris Johnson, new information suggests an Iranian missile may have brought down Ukraine International Airlines flight PS752 which crashed shortly after leaving Imam Khomeini Airport in Tehran on 8th January.

Speaking about information relating to the crash, Mr Johnson said there is now 'a body of information that the flight was shot down' by an Iranian missile and that the shooting down of the plane 'may well have been unintentional'.

Iran has ruled out a missile strike as the cause of the crash. In a statement, U.K. Prime Minister Boris Johnson said that the U.K. government was working with Canada and other nations affected by the crash:

> *'It is vital that there should be an immediate and respectful*
> *repatriation of those who've lost their lives to allow their*
> *families to grieve properly'.*

Canadian Prime Minister Justin Trudeau has also said he has seen evidence which suggested Iranian missiles brought down the jet. According to reports, U.S. satellites also detected two missile launches a short period before the explosion of the Ukrainian aircraft.

15th | Russia

The whole of the Russian government, including Prime Minister Dmitry Medvedev, have resigned.

The surprising move came just hours after Russian President Vladimir Putin proposed significant changes to the constitution while delivering his annual state–of–the–nation address.

Proposals made by President Putin could see a shift in the balance of power in Russia. In particular, the State Duma (the lower house of Parliament) would be granted the power to appoint the prime minister and members of the Cabinet, where this is currently done by the president. Putin argued that the president should retain the right to dismiss the prime minister and cabinet ministers. Any changes to the constitution must be put to a national vote, according to Putin.

The resignations have been accepted, but ministers have been asked to remain in a caretaker government until a new one can be formed.

Mr Medvedev is to be appointed as deputy head of the Presidential Security Council. He served as President of Russia between 2008 & 2012 and has been prime minister ever since.

16th | United States

President Donald Trump's impeachment trial has begun in the United States Senate, the first trial in more than two decades and only the third trial in American history.

The president was impeached by the House of Representatives in December 2019 following a telephone conversation between Trump and the Ukrainian President, Volodymr Zelensky, in July 2019. Trump is alleged to have asked Mr Zelensky to announce an investigation into Hunter Biden – the son of Joe Biden – for his role as a director in a Ukrainian oil company.

The impeachment trial is conducted in the same way as a traditional criminal court trial with a prosecution made up of Congressmen (known as managers) seeking to secure a conviction, whilst the president will have a team of defence lawyers. The Senate will vote either to convict or acquit the President; if two thirds vote to convict, the president is removed from office.

The only other presidents to be impeached – Bill Clinton, for lying under oath and obstruction of justice, and Andrew Johnson, for 11 separate high crime and misdemeanours – were both acquitted in the Senate trial, the latter by just a single vote.

At the time, Ukraine were hoping to receive $400m in military aid from the U.S., which Donald Trump was allegedly attempting to use as leverage.

18th | United Kingdom

Following the infamous 'Sandringham Summit' on the 13th of January, where the Royal Family worked out the formalities of 'Megxit', the royals have released a statement stating that the Duke and Duchess of Sussex will no longer be active members of the Royal Family.

It was also announced that they will lose their HRH titles in what has been described as a 'hard–Megxit' deal.

It is also expected that they discussed more details of the couple's future relationship with the Royal Family after they leave the family, as well as the financial arrangements that the couple are currently a part of.

19th | United Kingdom

The U.K. Government has this week announced plans to mark Brexit Day on the 31st of January.

A countdown clock is to be projected onto Downing Street ahead of the 23:00 departure time from the European Union, while Prime Minister Boris Johnson is to give an address to the nation on the same night. A special 50p coin to mark the departure from the E.U. will be released into circulation following 'Brexit Day', and various locally organised events can be expected to take place. A Cabinet meeting is also expected to be held in the North of England on the day.

Despite a crowdfunding campaign, Big Ben will not chime to mark the occasion. More than £200,000 had been raised of the £500,000 thought to be needed to cover the costs of operating the bell whilst the Elizabeth Tower is undergoing refurbishment, but the House of Commons authorities said that the cost could not be justified. The House of Commons Commission also raised concerns over the use of public donations to fund the event.

Conservation works on Big Ben began in 2017 and are set to continue until 2021. The famous clock has only chimed on scheduled special occasions since the works began.

20th | Yemen

A missile strike in Yemen on Saturday (20th) has killed at least 111 people and left many more injured.

The missile strike hit a military training camp in Marib, where soldiers had been gathering for evening prayers; it is the deadliest attack during the Yemen Civil War, that began in late–2014, to date.

The Yemen crisis is currently considered to be one of the worst humanitarian crises currently afflicting the globe, with estimates of more than 100,000 being killed in the past five years.

In Yemen, the major crisis is not just the ongoing civil war, with the Houthis fighting against Saudi–backed forces loyal to the government, but a far larger humanitarian disaster.

It is believed that there are as many as 11 million people struggling to access food, with a quarter of million living under famine conditions, meaning that they are on the borderline of sustenance.

It is believed that more than 80% of the total Yemeni population are in need of assistance, with water contamination, starvation and disease, causing devastation to the population.

There are reports of the Houthi forces confiscating food from the population, as well as poisoning water supplies.

The Saudi–backed government forces have placed a blockade around Yemen, starving the population of food supplies in order to pressure the rebel forces; the impact has mostly been felt by the civilian population. They have also led bombing campaigns of major infrastructure, making it harder for aid workers to provide support to the civilian population.

22nd | Greece

Greece has its first female president, Katerina Sakellaropoulou.

The former high court judge and human rights activist was elected to succeed Prokopis Pavlopoulos by the Hellenic Parliament, a significant moment for the country.

The Greek president is more of a national figurehead for the country, akin to the president of Germany, and it is the prime minister who carries out the day–to–day duties of government.

Throughout her career, Sakellaropoulou has broken through glass ceilings, with her also being the first female president of the Council of State, Greece's top court. Her election to the presidency marks another significant moment in a country that has often been criticised for failing to tackle gender gaps. There are hopes that Sakellaropoulou will be able to make significant strides whilst in office in advancing women's rights.

She was elected with 261 votes of a 300–seat assembly and will take office next month.

23rd | China

The city of Wuhan has gone into lockdown amid the outbreak of a virus that has left an estimated 18 dead in the Hubei province region of China.

More than 500 cases have been confirmed in the Hubei province, with a number of cases also reported in Vietnam and Singapore, which appear to have originated in Wuhan.

The virus is a new strain of coronavirus, which is currently believed to have originated at a wet–market in Wuhan, although this is disputed and the actual source is unknown. International health agencies have urged the Chinese government to give them access to the region in order to locate the original source and conduct research into how the disease can be combatted.

Questions have arisen as to how easy it will be to ensure the lockdown is effective, with Wuhan having a population of more than 11 million people and many already believed to have travelled away from the region since restrictions were announced. There are significant fears that it may already be too late to stop the virus spreading throughout the region, in a similar way to SARS in the early 2000s.

24th | United Kingdom

The U.K. government has held a meeting of its emergency COBRA committee in Whitehall to discuss the novel coronavirus outbreak; the prime minister was not in attendance.

At this stage, there are no confirmed cases of the virus in the U.K., with nine people awaiting results. Leaflets and information are being distributed at some U.K. airports about the virus, which has already spread to other countries, including Japan, Thailand, and the U.S.

China has introduced travel restrictions affecting around 20 million people across 10 cities as part of efforts to prevent and slow down the virus's spread.

The virus, known officially as 2019–nCoV, had not previously been identified in humans until last month. The virus is a new strain of the Coronavirus; in the early 2000s, another strain of coronavirus, the SARS (Severe Acute Respiratory Syndrome) virus, killed nearly 800 people throughout Asia, left thousands more sick, and resulted in a significant economic crash and left millions in fear. There are concerns that the new virus could have an equally devastating impact on the region.

At the moment, there is no treatment available to protect people against the virus.

24th | United Kingdom

Live facial recognition cameras will be used operationally by the Metropolitan Police for the first time on London streets, it has been announced.

The police force previously ran trials of facial recognition cameras in the capital, and it is hoped that the cameras will identify suspects wanted for serious and violent crimes. It is thought that the system could also be used to aid searches for missing persons.

Cameras are to be signposted and only used in certain targeted areas for around five to six hours at a time. However, the use of the cameras will likely prove controversial. Privacy campaigners have already described the plans as a 'serious threat to civil liberties' and have vowed to launch legal challenges against its use.

The Metropolitan Police has said that the technology is 'tried–and–tested', but privacy campaign group Big Brother Watch has said the plans represent 'an enormous expansion of the surveillance state and a serious threat to civil liberties in the U.K.'.

There are also fears about racial biases built into facial recognition algorithms, with many Twitter users citing studies that the technology often engrains the stereotypes fed into them, with a veneer of technology making the biases less apparent, but more pervasive.

24th | Lebanon

After months of protests at government corruption, a new government has taken office, following the resignation of Sad Hairi late last year.

The new government will be led by Hassan Diab, with the ministers in government being cut to one third of its original size. It is hoped that the smaller number will lead to more efficient leadership and help the country to arrest the ongoing economic and political crises that had led to the protests.

25th | United Kingdom

Prime Minister Boris Johnson has said the U.K. can now 'move forward as one country' as he signed the E.U. Withdrawal Agreement that is set to see the U.K. leave the E.U. next week.

Mr Johnson signed the document just hours after President of the European Commission, Ursula Von Der Leyen, and head of the European Council, Charles Michel, also signed the deal.

The deal must now be approved by the European Parliament. If the deal is approved, the U.K. should be leaving the European Union next Friday (31st).

The U.K. and E.U. still need to negotiate a future relationship and trade agreement, and this can be done after leaving day once the transition period has begun. While in the transition period, the U.K. will still be part of the Single Market and Customs Union, so no immediate disruption is expected; however, the U.K. will no longer have a seat in the European Parliament or European Council, two of the union's biggest decision-making bodies.

The transition period is currently set to run up until the end of the year; it may be extended; however, Boris Johnson has so far refused to publicly contemplate an extension.

26th | United States

Basketball superstar Kobe Bryant has been killed in a helicopter crash in California.

Bryant, along with eight others, was killed when the helicopter came down north of Los Angeles – his 13–year–old daughter Gianna was among those killed in the crash.

Born in 1978, Kobe Bryant was one of the most successful basketball players in history, winning the NBA on five occasions, as well as being an 18x NBA All–Star – featuring every year between 2000 and 2016.

Bryant was the youngest player ever to pass the career 30,000–point milestone and retired having shot 33,643 throughout his career – the third highest in history.

He was best known for donning the gold of the L.A. Lakers, a team he joined in the late 1990s, playing alongside the 7'1' Shaquille O'Neal, another of the sport's greatest stars, with the pair leading the lakers to the NBA title in 2000, 2001 and 2002.

The turn of the 2010s was the peak of Bryant's career, starring in one of the greatest sides in the NBA and securing back–to–back titles as the leading figure in one of the sport's historic brands.

Yet 2010 was to be the last of his NBA titles, with Kobe Bryant picking up a number of injuries in the subsequent years and the L.A. Lakers seeing their star wain. Kobe was also seeing his status as Basketball's main man fall, with Lebron James starring in the same team as Bryant for the 2012 Olympics, with James leading the United States' charge for the gold medal.

He retired in 2016, once again making the All–Star team and playing in his 18th All Star game.

28th | United Kingdom

The United Kingdom's government has approved technology made by Chinese company Huawei to create the country's 5G network, a controversial decision that has raised security fears.

Boris Johnson reportedly made the decision personally, despite fears that have seen the United States ban the use of the company's technology for the creation of their 5G network.

It has been raised that Huawei could pose a national security risk in building the nation's 5G infrastructure, with the company linked with the Chinese government. The United States has threatened to terminate intelligence sharing with the U.K. if they pressed ahead with the intention to permit Huawei.

Huawei will however be excluded from sensitive functions, with the U.K.'s National Cyber Security Centre reportedly telling other 'high–risk' vendors that Huawei are to be excluded from these functions.

30th | Switzerland

The World Health Organisation (WHO) has declared the outbreak of the novel coronavirus a global emergency.

The outbreak has continued to spread throughout China, so far leaving at least 170 people dead. Tedros Adhanom Ghebreyesus, Director–General of the WHO said;

> 'The main reason for this declaration is not what is happening in China but what is happening in other countries'.

Outside of China, there have been 98 cases of the virus confirmed in 18 different countries.

Dr Tedros praised the 'unprecedented response' by Chinese authorities to prevent the outbreak from spreading and said that the declaration of a global emergency was 'not a vote of no confidence in China'.

There have been six other Public Health Emergencies of International Concern (PHIE) declared by the World Health Organisation since 2009, including the swine flu pandemic, the polio declaration, the Zika virus epidemic and the Ebola virus outbreaks.

31st | United Kingdom

3 years, 7 months and 8 days since the E.U. referendum, the U.K. will leave the E.U. tonight – at 23:00 (GMT).

A 'Brexit Celebration' is to be held in Parliament Square between 21:00 and 23.15, hosted by the *Leave Means Leave* campaign group, backed by Brexit Party leader Nigel Farage.

U.K. embassies around the world have been warned against holding any special events to mark the U.K.'s exit from the E.U., over fears of any 'triumphalism' being badly received by the respective host countries of the embassies, and with many Britons not feeling it right to celebrate.

FEBRUARY

1st | United Kingdom

It has been confirmed that two cases of the novel coronavirus have been found in the United Kingdom.

One of the two people who tested positive for novel coronavirus is a student at the University of York. The university remains open as usual.

The student is one of two people in the U.K. confirmed to have the virus. Both persons are part of the same family and are understood to have fallen ill while at the Stay City Apartment Hotel in York. According to reports, the pair recently travelled to the U.K. from China.

The hotel, which was put into lockdown, has been thoroughly disinfected and is now open for business with there being a 'minimum ongoing risk of infection' according to officials.

The director of the National Infection Service at Public Health England, Professor Sharon Peacock, told the press that people who have come into close contact with the confirmed cases of the virus in the U.K. are being traced in an effort to minimise any risk to those people and the wider public. The health authority is defining close contact as being within 2 metres of an infected person for 15 minutes.

The pair infected with the virus are being treated at a specialist hospital unit, the Airborne High Consequences Infectious Disease Centre (HCID) at Newcastle's Royal Victoria Infirmary (RVI) hospital.

At this stage, cases of the coronavirus have been confirmed in at least 25 countries worldwide, but the only deaths from the virus have been in China.

3rd | United Kingdom

Journalists walked out of a Downing Street press briefing after the prime minister's director of communications attempted to restrict the briefing to only certain publications and broadcasters.

19

The briefing was regarding the Prime Minister Boris Johnson's Brexit plans, in particular, plans to negotiate a Canadian–style free trade agreement with the European Union.

On arrival at Downing Street, the journalists were split into two groups, with one group being asked to leave. The events resulted in all the journalists refusing to take part in the briefing and leaving 10 Downing Street.

Tensions had been increasing between Downing Street and the media in recent weeks, with Downing Street banning government ministers from appearing on BBC Radio 4's Today programme.

During the 2019 General Election, the Conservatives refused to attend multiple interviews and debates and dropped out of others. The prime minister's planned grilling on the Andrew Neil Show never went ahead, and an ice sculpture replaced him during a Channel 4 climate change debate that he pulled out of. More infamously, the prime minister was led into an industrial refrigeration unit when ambushed by reporters during a campaign milk round.

3rd | China

A number of temporary hospitals have been opened in China to deal with the patients that have contracted the novel coronavirus within the Hubei province.

The hospitals, some of which are converted conference centres, are set to house patients of the virus, as well as their families and other people that are required to quarantine as a result of the outbreak. Some other hospitals have been constructed in just a matter of days.

The hope is that the hospitals will help the Hubei province contain the spread of the virus and ease capacity on the other hospitals within the area, preventing a more profound public health crisis.

3rd | South Africa

An arrest warrant has been issued for 77–year–old former South African president, Jacob Zuma.

The former president was ousted in 2018 and is currently believed to be in Cuba receiving medical treatment. There is currently no extradition treaty between the countries and it is unclear whether Zuma will return to the country to face these charges.

The warrant has been issued for corruption charges that were allegedly committed whilst he was in office.

4th | United Kingdom

British nationals are being advised to leave China as the novel coronavirus outbreak continues.

The U.K. Foreign & Commonwealth Office have updated their travel advice to say 'If you're in China and able to leave, you should do so. '

In a statement, Foreign Secretary Dominic Raab said:

'The safety and security of British people will always be our top priority,'

'As such, we now advise British nationals in China to leave the country if they can, to minimise their risk of exposure to the virus'.

Britons are also being advised to avoid 'all but essential travel' to mainland China.

The Foreign Office is continuing to arrange the evacuation of any remaining Britons from the Hubei province, it is understood. Restrictions on movements are in place in large parts of China as they try to respond to the virus outbreak. Commercial flights are currently available from other parts of China away from the Hubei province.

The U.K. government recently announced it was moving non−essential embassy staff out of the region, to try and prevent them from exposure to the virus.

4th | Israel

Israeli President Benjamin Netanyahu has been indicted on corruption charges, though it is likely he will not face a court room any time soon.

The news came just hours before he was set to meet with President Trump about the United States' Middle East peace plan, although this is still expected to go ahead.

Netanyahu has been charged with fraud and bribery, although it is unlikely that there will be any conclusion to the charges for years.

5th | United States

President Donald Trump has been acquitted by the Senate of obstructing Congress and abusing the power of his office as president.

The vote in the Senate on Wednesday brought to an end Trump's impeachment trial and sees him remain in office. Trump has said that he will make a statement tomorrow 'to discuss our country's victory on the impeachment hoax'. The president has long denied any wrongdoing and has repeatedly referred to the impeachment process as a 'witch–hunt'.

The Senate, with the Republican Party holding the majority, voted almost entirely along partisan lines; he was acquitted 52–48 on the charge of 'abuse of power' and 53–47 on 'obstruction of Congress', deciding not to convict the president. Mitt Romney was the only Republican to vote to convict the president on the first article and no Republicans voted against the president on the second.

8th | Republic of Ireland

Irish Taoiseach (equivalent to prime minister), Leo Varadkar, has been defeated in the country's General Election, with his party finishing in third place and the incumbent only narrowly retaining his own seat.

The election, somewhat unusually held on a Saturday, returned a surprising result. No party gained overall power and created a situation where even a two–party coalition would fail to command a majority in the Dáil (Irish Parliament) and lack the votes to govern effectively.

Sinn Féin topped the popular vote and gained 37 seats (up from 22 in the 2016 poll), whilst Fianna Fáil returned the most seats with 38, coming second in the popular vote.

Fine Gael, the party of incumbent Taoiseach, Leo Varadkar – the first openly gay Irish leader – only managed to secure 35 seats, coming third in both the popular vote and seats won.

A number of smaller parties also gained seats in the Dáil, with the Greens gaining 9 seats on their 2016 result, to have 12, and the Social Democrats gaining four more seats, totalling 6.

The election was the first held using new constituency boundaries drawn up using the 2016 census, and saw the Dáil increase the number of seats to 160 (up from 158) – the impact of these changes on the election outcome is unclear.

Sinn Féin are a nationalist party and support the reunification of the island of Ireland. Their popular vote victory could mark a potentially significant moment in the history of both the Republic of Ireland and Northern Ireland if they are able to hold influence in the coalition government that is likely to form in the coming months. The leader of Sinn Féin, Mary Lou McDonald, said that she wanted to see a referendum on the reunification of Ireland within five years following her popular vote victory; despite winning the popular vote they still received just 24.5% of the total votes cast.

It is likely that, as the largest party in the new Dáil, Fianna Fáil's leader, Michaél Martin, will become the new Irish Taoiseach, provided that he can form an effective coalition government with other parties in the coming weeks.

10th | United Kingdom

Four more people in the U.K. are confirmed to have been infected by the novel coronavirus.

The announcement was made by the Chief Medical Officer for England, Professor Chris Whitty.

In a statement, Whitty said;

> *'The new cases are all known contacts of a previously confirmed U.K. case, and the virus was passed on in France'.*

The patients are understood to have been transferred to specialist NHS centres in London.

One of the eight people diagnosed in the U.K. caught the virus in Singapore, before travelling to France; he was diagnosed in Brighton, is being treated in London, and has been linked to five of the other cases. Two of the people diagnosed are healthcare workers.

A GP practice in Brighton has been temporarily closed, due to a staff member being diagnosed with the virus.

The announcement came as the Department of Health described the deadly virus as a 'serious and imminent threat' to public health. The description is though thought to have been used mainly for legal reasons – new powers have been given to help enforce quarantines of those who may be infected by the virus. The department has insisted the risk to individuals is low.

There have now been over 900 deaths in China from the virus.

10th | China

A number of hospitals set up in Wuhan, China, in order to deal with the novel coronavirus outbreak, have since been shut down, due to a lack of patients.

It was reported that 10 new hospitals had been set up to deal with the number of patients contracting the virus, but the majority of these have since been closed; more than 12,000 people are believed to have been treated in these hospitals since they opened in January – although many started to be closed within just weeks of opening.

The move to open these facilities was praised by the World Health Organisation who said that the move was likely effective in changing the course of a rapidly growing epidemic.

This also follows around 42,600 healthcare professionals from around China being sent to the Hubei province region to contain the pandemic.

11th | United Kingdom

In an era of 'populist' politics, politicians always claim to be connected to 'the people'. Some claim to appreciate their feelings. Some claim to be different from their colleagues. Others promise to 'Get Brexit Done'.

Then, there is Rory Stewart.

The London Mayoral election candidate and former Conservative leadership contender has launched a campaign where he is asking Londoners to invite him into their homes for a sleepover.

Launching #ComeKipWithMe, Mr Stewart tweeted;

> *'Today I'm launching #ComeKipWithMe – asking Londoners*
> *to invite me into their homes and show me the city through*
> *their eyes. I want to know your concerns and your ideas. And I*
> *promise to bring a sleeping bag and a box of chocolates!'*
> *@RoryStewartU.K.*

In a video, Stewart acknowledged 'it's a weird request' but said that walking through every borough was the only way mayors could get to know their cities.

Rory Stewart had previously gained notoriety for his #RoryWalks campaigning for the Conservative leadership, where he would pop up in random areas of the country and invite people to chat with him. The novel approach to campaigning was inspired by his previous career as a diplomat and traveller; walking across Afghanistan and other regions for months on end. He later documented some of his travels in award–winning books, *The Places In Between* (2004) and *The Marches* (2015).

Mr Stewart was amongst the MPs suspended from the Conservative Party in 2019 for voting against Boris Johnson's Brexit deal, later stepping down as a Conservative MP before the 2019

General Election; instead running to take over Johnson's old gig as the Mayor of London.

The launch of his strangest campaigning idea yet has sparked a mixed reaction on social media.

11th | Switzerland

What's in a name? Apparently, the virus strain and the year in which it emerged. The world health organisation has officially named the novel coronavirus as COVID–19 – meaning Coronavirus Disease 2019.

The virus, previously known as the novel coronavirus or SARS–CoV–2, has been given an official name, which allows it to be separated and distinguished from other strains of coronavirus more easily.

Viruses are named after their genetic structure, making it easier for scientists to develop diagnostic tests, vaccines and medicines that can aid in the fight against the disease.

13th | United Kingdom

A significant reshuffle of the Cabinet has taken place, with multiple ministers being sacked and Sajid Javid resigning from his role as Chancellor.

A reshuffle of the Cabinet had been expected, but it was widely thought that most key ministers would remain in their posts. It is understood that Mr Javid was asked to sack all his advisers in an effort to bring the Treasury closer to 10 Downing Street, but he refused and resigned from the government instead.

Rishi Sunak, the Conservative MP for Richmond (Yorks) is to replace Mr Javid as chancellor of the exchequer. Mr Sunak has significantly less experience than Mr Javid did when he entered the role as chancellor; however, he has served as the chief secretary to the treasury since July 2019.

The resignation of the now former chancellor could throw into question the date of next month's scheduled budget and see No. 10 exerting much more control over the Chancellor's operations and his team in No. 11 Downing Street.

The Cabinet reshuffle seems to have shown Boris Johnson choose power over people, with many ministers sacked who may have been considered not to be completely loyal to the prime minister. Boris Johnson has a substantial majority in Parliament, but will still not want a divided Cabinet, especially in a time of considerable challenges for the government on Brexit, health, crime, transport and the environment.

16th | United Kingdom

There has been severe flooding throughout much of the United Kingdom after Storm Dennis ripped through the heart of the country.

The Midlands were reported to be amongst the worst hit, with a major incident being declared in the East Midlands village of Lowdham.

Towns around Leicestershire were also badly impacted, with many homes being flooded after the River Soar broke its banks.

Wales have also been badly impacted by the floods, with the country being hit on the 14th of February, before the storm moved towards England. Flooding around parts of northern and southern Wales was particularly bad, with Pontypridd and Cardiff being impacted when the River Taff recorded the highest water levels in its history.

Storm Dennis came after Storm Ciara had also caused floods and widespread disruption to public transport services across much of the U.K. the previous weekend.

19th | France

Don't get sick in France – it's illegal!

In fairness, it is not illegal across the whole of France; a number of mayors across rural France have sardonically banned falling ill in an attempt to highlight a lack of doctors and the potential dangers for local residents.

Rural areas are struggling to receive adequate healthcare according to the mayors and the fears of the novel coronavirus are leading them to take drastic action.

25th | Italy

The COVID–19 outbreak is continuing to worsen, with the virus spreading across more European countries.

11 elderly people have so far died from the virus in Italy, while cases of the virus have recently been confirmed in Spain, Austria, Switzerland and Croatia.

The U.K. Foreign & Commonwealth Office has updated its travel advice, saying it advises 'against all but essential travel' to 10 small towns in Lombardy and one in Veneto. The towns usually attract tourists for their ski resorts but have been put into lockdown due to the COVID–19 outbreak.

Meanwhile, some schools in England and Northern Ireland have shut for deep cleaning after students and staff returned from skiing trips in the region.

The majority of cases of the COVID–19 outbreak are still in China, where over 70,000 cases have been reported so far. While the number of cases confirmed in China is high, the number of new diagnoses has generally been falling, and Chinese officials say that more than 18,500 people have recovered from the virus. It is thought that the elderly and those with underlying health conditions are most at risk.

29th | Afghanistan

A conditional peace agreement has been signed between the United States and the Taliban.

The agreement was signed in Doha, Qatar and will see the United States begin to remove troops from the country in the coming months, with President Trump promising to remove 5,000 troops by May.

This is not an end to the war and the United States are not fully withdrawing, but it is a significant de–escalation of the U.S.'s presence in the country.

It is expected that talks between the Taliban and the Afghanistan government will continue in the coming months.

29th | United Kingdom

Prime Minister Boris Johnson and fiancée Carrie Symonds have announced that they are engaged and that the couple are expecting a baby in the summer.

The couple got engaged at the end of 2019 and made the announcement on Saturday.

Ms Symonds, 31, wrote on Instagram that she and Mr Johnson, 55, became engaged at the end of last year, saying 'Many of you already know but for my friends that still don't, we got engaged at the end of last year... and we've got a baby hatching early summer. Feel incredibly blessed'.

This is set to be Mr Johnson's third marriage after he divorced his first wife in 1993 and separated from his second wife Marina Wheeler in 2018.

29th | United Kingdom

The Home Office's top civil servant, Sir Philip Rutnam has resigned and is threatening to sue the government.

Mr Rutnam said he had 'been the target of a vicious and orchestrated briefing campaign'. He has said he plans to pursue a claim against the government for constructive dismissal – whereby an employer has committed a serious breach of contract, entitling the employee to resign.

In a statement published by the BBC, Mr Rutnam said 'I have this morning resigned as permanent secretary'. I take this decision with great regret after a career of 33 years'. He added, 'It has been alleged that I have briefed the media against the home secretary. This — along with many other claims — is completely false'.

The departure of Mr Rutnam comes following reports of severe tensions between Mr Rutnam and Priti Patel, the Home Secretary. Sir Philip said that it was his duty to 'protect the health, safety and wellbeing' of 35,000 Home Office workers, but his work had created tensions between him and the Home Secretary. He said that he had received allegations that Ms Patel's conduct towards employees at the government department had at times involved 'swearing, belittling people, making unreasonable and repeated demands'.

The head of the civil service, Sir Mark Sedwill said he had received the resignation 'with great regret'.

MARCH

3rd | United Kingdom

The U.K. government has published an action plan for dealing with the COVID–19 outbreak.

The plans say that police could be reduced to just dealing with very serious crimes and maintaining public order in the event of a major coronavirus pandemic in the U.K. The NHS could also be closed to all but critical care patients, and the army may be drafted in to maintain public order if necessary.

The released document highlights plans for a 'reasonable worst case (RWC)' scenario, which outlines potential for a 3–day doubling rate and an overall fatality rate of up to 1% of the population. The extent to which the virus outbreak will impact the U.K. does, of course, remain uncertain.

There are currently more than 90,000 cases of the virus around the world and more than 3,000 deaths. In the U.K., there have been 51 confirmed cases of the virus.

The plan does not predict how many people could be infected if a coronavirus epidemic hit the U.K., but ministers have confirmed there could be an increase in deaths from the current outbreak. According to reports, four out of five people could contract the virus, and one in five workers could be absent during the weeks when the virus peaked.

So far, evidence has suggested that those with pre–existing health conditions and the elderly may be most at risk.

3rd | United Kingdom

In a press conference discussing the COVID–19 outbreak, Prime Minister Boris Johnson attempted to alleviate fears about the potential impact on people's lives by stating that he was shaking hands with hospital patients.

29

He said that he had recently visited a hospital where he thought there were 'a few coronavirus patients', before going on to say 'I shook hands with everybody, you'll be pleased to know'.

The prime minister also urged people to make up their own minds about what they feel comfortable doing, before Chief Scientific Advisor Sir Patrick Vallance cut across the prime minister and urged the public to 'wash your hands'.

Earlier in the day, the government's Scientific Advisory Group for Emergencies (SAGE) committee had advised against hand–shaking and other forms of close greetings in an effort to stop the spread of the virus.

Boris Johnson's spokesperson said that the prime minister would not have seen the advice before the press conference and, after seeing the advice, would change his behaviour accordingly.

To date, there have been 55 confirmed cases of COVID–19 in the U.K. and no fatalities.

4ᵗʰ | United States

With the vote still being counted in California, former vice–president Joe Biden has taken the lead in the 14 states that voted on 'Super Tuesday' – day where the most states take part in the primary – and wrestled a lead in total the Democratic primary delegate count.

Primaries are a method of the major parties choosing who their presidential candidate will be, with voters in each state getting to vote for which candidate they want to be the party's nominee in the November election.

Following a rough showing for Biden in the first 3 states, where Senator Bernie Sanders was able to hold a delegate lead, Biden was able to pull ahead with a decisive victory in South Carolina – the first state with a significant African American base, to vote.

His victory there helped propel him to victory in many states on Super Tuesday.

All told, Biden won 10 states: Texas, Oklahoma, North Carolina, Alabama, Virginia, Tennessee, Minnesota, Massachusetts, Arkansas and most likely Maine, while Sanders only won Utah, Vermont, Colorado and California.

While Sanders is not out of the race yet, Biden's win does point to a visible shift in who is favoured to go to the convention in July – where the party officially picks its nominee – with the most votes.

Following a terrible showing, former New York mayor, Michael Bloomberg – winning only the territory of American Samoa – dropped out of the race in order to endorse Biden; only Biden, Sanders and senator Elizabeth Warren remain as major contenders in the race. With Warren's poor showing in the early primaries, winning no states, and coming third in her home state, it is unclear if she has any path to the nomination.

Despite another defeat, Warren said she is planning on staying in the race. If she does, it will almost certainly be to the detriment of Bernie Sanders, as Warren is also running as a progressive, and will continue to split the progressive vote, leaving a clearer path for Biden to take the Democratic nomination.

6th | United Kingdom

There are questions over how the continuing spread of the COVID–19 could impact workers in the U.K. and beyond.

There are 115 confirmed cases of COVID–19 in the U.K. so far, and one older person with pre–existing health conditions has died after contracting the virus. 97 cases in the U.K. are active, according to data, while 18 people have recovered.

This week at Prime Minister's Questions on Wednesday, Boris Johnson announced that workers will be able to get statutory sick pay from their first day off work under emergency coronavirus legislation. Usually, workers would only get the pay from their fourth day off work.

Johnson said that people who self–isolate to help protect other people from contracting the virus should not be 'penalised for doing the right thing'. Some people are currently being asked to self–isolate if they have visited one of the locations with a higher risk of contracting the virus.

The announcement could lead more people to self–isolate, which may help the U.K.'s effort to contain and delay the spread of the virus.

Boris Johnson suggested that those not eligible for the pay would be 'entitled to help through existing systems such as universal credit'. These comments were met with groans from the opposition benches in the House of Commons when announced. It is usually over a month before applicants to Universal Credit can receive any benefits, which may cause severe problems for vulnerable people and those struggling financially due to staying away from work while they have the coronavirus.

Some schools and workplaces, including in Canary Wharf, have already been evacuated due to concerns over a case of the coronavirus amongst staff, with employees advised to work from home where possible. Where staff are unable to work from home, there could be significant logistical challenges for businesses, adding to problems caused by the virus' impact on the economic climate.

8th | United Kingdom

U.K. supermarkets have started rationing some essential food and household supplies due to consumers stockpiling as a result of coronavirus fears.

The U.K.'s largest supermarket chain, Tesco, is placing purchase limits on some items in-store and online, including antibacterial gels and wipes, as well as pasta and some tinned vegetables. Customers will be limited to buying no more than five of each item.

The restrictions are in effect nationwide but may vary in some areas. Similar restrictions have been placed by Waitrose online, while Boots and Asda have restricted sales on some hand sanitisers to a maximum of two per person. Online supermarket Ocado has also put limits on the purchase of some items, including toilet roll.

People have been allegedly stockpiling items to resell online at a high mark-up, with fears that the pandemic could result in significant inflation if supply lines are impacted due to lockdowns throughout the world.

Photos emerged this week of members of the public 'panic buying' amid coronavirus fears, with empty shelves in toilet paper and pasta aisles emerging, only further fuelling panic amongst shoppers.

The government has told consumers not to 'panic buy'; however, it would appear that many are doing the opposite. The Competition and Markets Authority (CMA) has also told suppliers to be responsible after Facebook and Amazon cracked down on items such as hand gels and face masks being sold online at hugely marked-up prices.

9th | Italy

Italy, one of the countries to be suffering worst from the COVID-19 outbreak, has extended strict quarantine measures nationwide, becoming the first nation to institute a national lockdown.

Cases of the virus have now been confirmed in all 20 Italian regions, with the country's death toll from the virus jumping to 463 on

Monday. There have been over 7,800 cases of the virus in the country so far.

New restrictions are due to come into effect today, which will see members of the public only permitted to travel if they can prove they are doing so for work or in the case of family emergencies. All schools and universities are already closed in the country, and some areas already have strict quarantine measures in place. A variety of public venues including cinemas and gyms will remain closed.

There are controls at train stations and restrictions at some airports and ports. In a televised address, Italian Prime Minister Giuseppe Conte urged Italians to stay at home and said;

'We're having an important growth in infection... and of deaths'.

'This is why I decided to adopt even more strong and severe measures to contain the advance... and protect the health of all citizens'.

All sporting events and public gatherings are being banned in the country. Weddings and funerals are banned and bars and restaurants will be forced to close at 6 pm.

Italy is the country currently suffering worst from the virus outbreak behind China. Worldwide, there have been over 114,000 cases of the virus confirmed, with over 4,000 deaths.

11th | United Kingdom

Nadine Dorries, a health minister, has become the first member of the government to contract coronavirus.

She is said to be isolating at home and is currently not experiencing any symptoms.

A number of individuals with whom she has been in contact have also been asked to self– isolate, including Labour MP Rachel Maskell, who had met with Dorries in recent days.

It is believed that she may have been in contact with other members of the government in recent days, including the prime minister; however, they are not isolating at this time.

12th | United States

President Donald Trump has announced a travel ban amid the coronavirus outbreak.

The restrictions ban people from much of Europe from entering the United States, in a bid to prevent the further spread of the COVID–19 coronavirus.

President Trump accused Europe of spreading the 'foreign virus' to the U.S. and said Europe had 'failed to take the same precautions [as the U.S.]' and restrict travel from China and other hotspots.

There are 1,135 confirmed cases of the virus throughout the United States so far, with 38 deaths reported.

The ban, which is initially expected to last for 30 days, with flights from the 26 European countries in the Schengen zone to be banned – however, the U.K. and Ireland are not included in the ban. The ban applies to anyone who was in the Schengen Area during the 14 days before their attempted entry into the United States, so foreign nationals are unlikely to be able to reach the United States via the U.K.

Speaking from the Oval Office last night, President Trump said;

'To keep new cases from entering our shores, we will be suspending all travel from Europe'.

'We made a lifesaving move with early action on China' he added. 'Now we must take the same action with Europe'.

Trump also signed a Presidential Memorandum on making general use face masks available to healthcare workers.

Travel restrictions are designed to impact people only, not cargo and trade. U.S. citizens, permanent residents and their families are all excluded from the ban, as are health professionals involved in international efforts to combat the virus, diplomats and sea or aircrew.

It is unknown whether those booked onto flights to the United States from the Schengen Area will be able to receive compensation. Generally, airlines do not have to pay compensation if the reasons for a flight being cancelled are beyond their control – in this case, it would be in control of the United States administration.

Multiple countries and airlines had already suspended flights to certain destinations, including China and Italy, who are worst affected by the pandemic. Malta has banned travel with Germany, France, Spain, Switzerland and Italy in efforts to prevent the spread of the virus on the Mediterranean island.

13th | United Kingdom

The U.K. Local Elections and the London Mayoral Elections have been postponed amid the coronavirus outbreak; they will now take place in 2021.

Local elections were due to take place in the U.K. on Thursday 7 May, to elect candidates to seats on 118 English local councils and select mayors in eight areas, including London and Birmingham.

Following the announcement, it is unclear whether Rory Stewart will continue to sleep over at voter's houses.

13th | United Kingdom

Mass gatherings in the U.K. are set to be banned from next week under plans amid the coronavirus outbreak.

On Thursday, U.K. Prime Minister Boris Johnson stopped short of announcing major shutdowns, however, it is now believed that various types of public events will be banned. Many major sporting events have already been cancelled or postponed – including Euro 2020 and the Tokyo Olympics – and some public venues have closed their doors. Schools are being advised to remain open, however, some universities have cancelled all face–to–face teaching.

It has been reported that a source in Whitehall has said that the government has drafted emergency legislation to stop mass gatherings and to compensate organisations.

The government have been criticised in recent days for allowing a football match to go ahead with fans on Wednesday the 11th of March, with Spanish side Atletico Madrid travelling to the North West to face Liverpool.

Cheltenham racecourse gained similar criticism today after a horse racing event saw 70,000 in attendance, worrying to fears that it could have potentially exposed swathes of people to the virus, who will spread it further as they travel home.

16th | France

President Emmanuel Macron has announced increased travel restrictions amid the pandemic, with borders to close for 30 days.

The restrictions are to begin at noon on Tuesday. The French President also warned that 'movements will be very strongly reduced' for 15 days, saying the measures were necessary due to people not complying with earlier public health measures and advice to reduce the spread of the coronavirus.

French people on holiday will be able to travel back to France and those living abroad will be able to be repatriated.

Restrictions are expected to be introduced on how far people can travel from their homes and for what purpose. Transport is expected to be severely limited, and Macron has demanded that companies make it possible for all employees in France to work from home.

Macron also announced the government was looking into waiving some tax payments and that it would provide €300 billion in loans to companies who needed support.

16th | United States

The 11th debate of the 2020 Democratic primary was the first head–to–head of the cycle, with Bernie Sanders and Joe Biden the final two candidates vying for the Democratic Party nomination, in the backdrop of a growing global health crisis.

Dubbed the 'coronavirus debate', the candidates spent almost an hour discussing their responses to the crisis, suggesting what they would do to tackle the ongoing pandemic.

Describing the pandemic as a 'war', former vice–president Biden suggested he would utilise the military to put in place temporary hospitals and ensure that the U.S. healthcare system did not become overrun, before moving on to suggest that he would ensure the government would cover all healthcare costs.

Bernie Sanders went further and struck a more existential tone, suggesting that the reason for the difficulty America has had in reacting to the crisis is fuelled by a broken healthcare system, where many Americans, too scared of high healthcare costs, are putting off treatment and testing, potentially putting themselves and others at greater risk.

Sanders suggested that whilst a strong response is needed to the pandemic, specifically, the spread of coronavirus is indicative of a wider issue within the United States' healthcare system. Biden hit back, suggesting that a single–payer system has not helped to prevent the crisis across much of Europe, before suggesting that his healthcare plan, an extension of Obamacare, would be more effective and far easier to pass through Congress.

Despite a few slipups, Biden came through unscathed, largely settling many of fears about his capability to hold office; he could be in for more big wins in the next primary elections on Tuesday.

Whilst Biden has moved to support free college tuition for low–income Americans and has thrown his support behind Elizabeth Warren's bankruptcy bill, it is unlikely he has done enough to fully address Sanders' supporters' concerns.

Uniting these voters behind him will be crucial for the November election and the COVID–19 debate showed that doing so will not be an easy task.

16th | United States

The Dow Jones – a United States stock market index – has suffered the biggest single–day points collapse in history, defeating the previous record set just four days ago.

The Dow fell by nearly 1,997.10 points, with the coronavirus pandemic continuing to hit industry and businesses worldwide.

Although the Dow had been running high in 2020, with a number of tax breaks throughout the Trump presidency having a positive impact on the price of America's biggest companies, the fall is still a dramatic one. It makes it worse than any fall during the 1930 stock market crash, that lead to the Great Depression.

As one of the world's most valuable markets, the collapse in the Dow's aggregate price is a significant indicator of what is happening elsewhere, with the FTSE 100 in the U.K. also suffering from a similarly steep decline in recent weeks.

Markets are reacting to the fact that the coronavirus pandemic is looking increasingly likely to rip through the entire world, with countries failing to contain outbreaks.

Following a strong few years, the Dow Jones was running at close to 30,000 points – a historic high – however, the pandemic resulted in a single–day loss of 13% of the index's total value.

Stock markets are typically not a good indicator of a country's overall economic performance, failing to take account of how the economy is impacting individuals. However, it can be indicative of where the money is flowing and the confidence of investors in the economy overall; it can be an indicator of the economies' general health.

The decline in the Dow is likely to be a precursor to more significant economic decline throughout the United States – and global economy, with unemployment and business insolvency likely to grow as confidence in the economy wains.

18th | United Kingdom

All schools in England are to close at the end of the week to the vast majority of pupils amid the Coronavirus pandemic, it has been announced.

It had earlier been announced that schools in Scotland and Wales would be closing on Friday, with First Minister of Scotland Nicola Sturgeon warning that people should not assume that they will open again until the end of the summer term. Schools in Northern Ireland closed on Wednesday with immediate effect.

It is understood that schools can no longer continue as normal due to large numbers of staff self–isolating. Speaking in the House of Commons on Wednesday, Education Secretary Gavin Williamson said;

'After schools shut their gates on Friday afternoon, they will remain closed until further notice.

'This will be for all children, except for those of key workers and where children who are most vulnerable'.

Mr Williamson also advised independent and boarding schools to close. He added that a national voucher system would be set up for children eligible for free school meals.

U.K. Prime Minister Boris Johnson said that exams would not occur in May and June as planned, but alternative arrangements would instead be made to ensure students get the academic qualifications they deserve. He urged parents not to leave children with older relatives and grandparents as they may be more at risk from the virus.

19th | United Kingdom

Prime Minister Boris Johnson has reiterated that people should follow the advice given to help the U.K. respond to the COVID–19 coronavirus pandemic, saying that we can make a 'huge difference' if we all do follow the advice together.

Speaking during the daily coronavirus press conference from Downing Street on Thursday, U.K. Prime Minister Boris Johnson said;

'We can turn the tide in the next 12 weeks and we can send coronavirus packing if we all take the steps we have outlined'.

He warned that the 12–week timeline could not be certain and what would happen after 12 weeks could not be guaranteed at this time.

The prime minister said there is no prospect of the government wanting to stop public transport in London, but that people should avoid events and venues such as pubs and clubs where the virus could be transmitted. Mr Johnson thanked Britons for their efforts and for following the advice thus far, urging them to continue doing the same. He said there was evidence that people were following the advice, with there being much lower than usual takings in the retail and hospitality industries and for Transport for London.

Asked if the government would introduce stricter measures, Mr Johnson said that if the government considered that further measures were needed due to people not following advice, then they may be introduced. It was implied that options, including closing shops and restaurants, remained on the table.

The prime minister also urged members of the public to refrain from panic–buying and be reasonable when shopping.

Mr Johnson also said that negotiations are taking place to buy a 'so–called antibody test, as simple as a pregnancy test' that can show whether you have had the virus. He said;

> 'It is early days but if it works as its proponents claim, then we will buy literally hundreds of thousands of these kits as soon as practicable because obviously it has the potential to be a total game changer'.

It was added that these tests, if they work, would be rolled out to healthcare workers first and then other essential workers before the general public.

The prime minister also said that companies should stand behind their staff because the government would stand behind them. He added that further information on how the government would support companies and workers would be announced by Chancellor Rishi Sunak the next day.

20th | United Kingdom

All cafes, pubs, bars, restaurants and gyms must close from tonight, Prime Minister Boris Johnson has ordered.

Clubs, theatres, cinemas and leisure centres should also close their doors as the U.K. battles to respond to the COVID–19 outbreak. Takeaway food outlets will be able to remain open at this time.

The Prime Minister has urged people to stay at home, saying, 'your sacrifice means we are putting the country in a better and stronger position and we will be able to save thousands of lives'. However, he has stopped short of implementing a 'national lockdown' akin to that seen in Italy and increasingly throughout other parts of Europe.

20th | United Kingdom

U.K. Chancellor Rishi Sunak has announced an unprecedented list of measures to help employees and employers amid the challenging economic circumstances during the COVID–19 outbreak.

The measures set out in the government's 'Plan for People's Jobs and Incomes' will see the British government step in to help pay people's wages 'for the first time in our history', according to Mr Sunak.

Under the plans, government grants will cover 80% of the salaries of retained workers, up to a total of £2,500 a month. The scheme will be open to any employer in the country and will apply to wages backdated to March 1st 2020. There is no funding limit on the scheme, and it will be available before the end of April for at least 3 months.

The government is also offering support to struggling businesses through the coronavirus Business Interruption Loan Scheme, while the Universal Credit Standard Allowance and Working Tax Credit Basic Element will both increase for the next 12 months by £1,000 a year.

In a tweet on Friday evening, Mr Sunak said;

'We want to look back on this time and remember how, in the face of a generation–defining moment, we undertook a collective national effort – and stood together'.

23rd | United Kingdom

Boris Johnson has announced major new measures in the U.K.'s response to the COVID–19 pandemic during a televised address to the nation – England will effectively go into national lockdown, with the governments of Scotland, Wales and Northern Ireland taking similar measures.

Earlier in the day, the government introduced the Coronavirus Bill, which will give the government greater power to make laws and restrictions in order to combat the pandemic. Parliament will not have to give their consent to all of the restrictions and laws being passed by the government under the measures.

The prime minister has said that Britons must stay at home from this point forward, marking the start of the U.K.s lockdown. People can only leave home for the following reasons;

— Shopping for basic necessities, as little as possible
— One form of exercise a day
— A medical need
— To travel to work, but only where absolutely necessary

All shops that don't sell essential goods must close immediately, and other public venues, including libraries, will also close. All gatherings of more than 2 people are to be banned, and all social events, including weddings and baptisms, are to be banned (funerals excluded). Parks are to remain open, but police will have the powers to disperse crowds.

Police will have the powers to fine people for non–compliance against the new measures.

While not yet described as such by Downing Street, the measures effectively see a lockdown of the U.K., akin to those seen in Europe. Transport networks will not be shut down, but many are already operating reduced services. Reminding the country of the reason for the government's approach, Mr Johnson said;

'Coronavirus is the biggest threat this country has faced for decades'.

'If too many people become unwell at any given time, the NHS will be unable to handle it'.

The government said it would review the new measures in three weeks and relax them, but only if appropriate.

The comments came as the prime minister gave a special evening televised address to the nation. At the weekend, thousands of Brits were seen enjoying the sunshine, going against the social distancing measures previously set out.

23rd | United Kingdom

A campaign has been set up encouraging the whole of the U.K. to applaud the NHS to show support – all at the same time.

The Clap for Our Carers campaign is encouraging Britons to applaud NHS workers from the doorsteps of their homes, gardens, windows and balconies on Thursday, 26 March at 8 pm.

The idea behind the campaign is simple – to show appreciation for the doctors, nurses, GPs and all other types of health workers who are facing such challenging tasks during the pandemic.

Britons are being encouraged to live stream their participation on social media. Due to the virus, social distancing measures are being advised, so members of the public should ensure they stay at least 2 metres away from others while taking part. Similar campaigns have taken place in other countries around the world, including in Spain, France and Italy as citizens try to raise spirits amid the pandemic.

24th | United Kingdom

The U.K.'s Health Secretary Matt Hancock has said the government is seeking a quarter of a million volunteers to help the NHS during the pandemic.

Volunteers will need to be in good health and will help the NHS support vulnerable persons. Mr Hancock said;

> *'We are seeking a quarter of a million volunteers, people in good health to help the NHS, for shopping, for the delivery of medicines and to support those who are shielding to protect their own health'.*

The Health Secretary said 11,788 people had so far responded to a previous call for former NHS staff to return to the service, including 2600 doctors, 6,147 nurses and over 2,500 other professionals. He added that 5,550 final year medics and 18,700 final year student nurses would be joining the service on the frontline.

Mr Hancock has also said that a temporary makeshift hospital will open in the ExCeL Centre in London. The makeshift hospital will be called the Nightingale Hospital and will have two wards, both having the capacity for 2,000 people. The hospital will be set up with the help of the military.

The announcements came during Downing Street's daily coronavirus press briefing, which was held digitally for the first time.

Questions and concerns were raised during the press conference about some employees who considered their work to be non–essential but had been told by their employer that they had to come into work. Mr Hancock said the government would enforce the closure of the businesses and retailers that it had already set out.

Mr Hancock said the government had purchased 3 million antibody tests, which will be available very soon for patients and NHS staff. A new testing facility is opening in Milton Keynes today, and 7.5 million PPE items have been shipped in the last 24 hours.

27th | United Kingdom

U.K. Prime Minister Boris Johnson has tested positive for the COVID–19 coronavirus. In a tweet, Mr Johnson said;

> *'Over the last 24 hours I have developed mild symptoms and tested positive for coronavirus. I am now self–isolating, but I will continue to lead the government's response via video–conference as we fight this virus. Together will beat this. #StayHomeSaveLives'. @BorisJohnson*

In a video, Mr Johnson said he had developed mild symptoms, including a temperature and a persistent cough. He said; 'Be in no doubt that I can continue, thanks to the wizardry of modern technology, to communicate with all my top team to lead the national fightback against coronavirus'.

In a statement, Downing Street said the prime minister had been tested on the advice of Chief Medical Officer Professor Chris Whitty after he had been experiencing 'mild symptoms' on Thursday.

The prime minister was last seen outside of Downing Street on the 26th of March with the Chancellor Rishi Sunak, to take part in 'Clap for Our Carers'.

Johnson has not called on his deputy Dominic Raab at this time, although Raab could step up to carry out the Prime Minister's duties if he were incapacitated.

Shortly after the prime minister was reported to have returned a positive COVID–19 test, his Health Secretary, Matt Hancock and the United Kingdom's chief medical officer, Chris Whitty, also tested positive. Matt Hancock said that he would be self–isolating for 7 days and was experiencing mild symptoms, whilst Professor Whitty is also experiencing mild symptoms. This means that three of the country's top figures in fighting the virus will all be required to isolate and continue their duties from home.

29th | United Kingdom

A consultant working in Derby and Burton hospitals has died after testing positive for COVID–19, becoming the first frontline worker to die with COVID–19.

In a statement, NHS England said that Amged El–Hawrani, an ear, nose and throat (ENT) specialist, died aged 55 on Saturday evening at Leicester Royal Infirmary.

30th | Hungary

Hungary's Parliament has passed what has been described as an 'enabling act', in response to the coronavirus pandemic; the bill effectively removes any parliamentary oversight of President Viktor Orbán.

The act, gives Orbán almost completely unfettered control over the nation, without the need for Parliamentary oversight.

The government have defended their decision due to the necessities of the pandemic, with many other countries – including the United Kingdom – passing similar bills to ensure the government are able to deal with the pandemic efficiently.

However, the concern is that the bill will not lapse following the pandemic and will continue to give Orbán control over the country without oversight for years to come. The terms of the legislation are considered overly vague and, unlike in many other countries who have introduced similar legislation, are not time limited, potentially allowing powers to exist indefinitely.

APRIL

Virus Threatens Nations | Inspirational Fundraising

4th | United Kingdom

Sir Keir Starmer has been elected as the new leader of the Labour Party, replacing Jeremy Corbyn, who resigned following Labour's historic defeat in the 2019 General Election.

Starmer, who had served as Shadow Brexit Secretary and has been an MP since 2015, had been widely expected to win the three–month contest, topping polls throughout the race.

He beat out the competition from Rebecca Long–Bailey and Lisa Nandy. Starmer was elected in the first round of voting, gaining 275,780 votes (56.2%). Ms Long–Bailey came second with 135,218 votes (27.6%), while Ms Nandy came third with 79,597 votes (16.2%).

Angela Rayner has also been elected as the new Deputy Leader of the Labour Party, winning 52.6% of the vote after second and third preferences were added, bringing her over the majority threshold needed to win.

A special conference had been planned to unveil the winners of both the leadership and deputy leadership contests; however, it was cancelled due to the coronavirus pandemic. The results were instead announced on social media, slightly behind schedule, with the Labour Party website crashing at the time of the results being due (10:45 BST).

In his pre–recorded victory speech, Sir Keir said; 'It is the honour and the privilege of my life to be elected as leader of the Labour Party', acknowledging 'it comes at a moment like none other in our lifetime'.

The newly elected leader said the party was failing in its 'historic purpose' and pledged to lead the party to change and rethink where required. In his speech, he said;

> *'This is my pledge to the British people: I will do my utmost to guide us through these difficult times, to serve all of our communities and to strive for the good of our country. I will lead this greatly party into a new era with confidence and with hope, so that when the time comes, we can serve our country again, in government'.*

Sir Keir also addressed the topic of the COVID–19 pandemic and hinted that the Labour Party would be willing to work with the government in the national interest;

> *'Under my leadership, we will engage constructively with the government. Not opposition for opposition's sake. Not scoring party political points or making impossible demands, but with the courage to support, where that's the right thing to do'.*

> *'Our purpose when we do that is the same as the government's – to save lives and to protect our country – a shared purpose'.*

Starmer's election comes after Boris Johnson wrote to the leaders of all of the opposition parties to invite them to work together through 'this moment of national emergency'.

Starmer's election as Labour leader comes after Labour's heavy defeat at the General Election on 12 December 2019 – their worst performance since the Second World War. The Labour Party lost 59 seats, while the Conservatives gained 47 seats and a large majority, leading to the resignation of Jeremy Corbyn.

4th | United Kingdom

As many as a dozen 5G towers have been attacked throughout the United Kingdom in recent weeks, with conspiracy theorists claiming that they are causing coronavirus.

Although there is – unsurprisingly – no evidence for this, some conspiracy theorists are drawing a connection between 5G infrastructure, some of which is being built by Chinese company Huawei, and the coronavirus, which originated in China. This has resulted in at least a dozen towers being attacked, with a number of them being set on fire.

With the videos being shared on social media, many have been encouraging more people to join their attacks on 5G towers, with some suggesting that it is the only way to defeat coronavirus.

The companies affected, primarily Vodafone, EE and Three, have urged people to stop burning the towers and cited the lack of any scientific evidence of a connection between the metal 5G towers and the biological virus that is killing people throughout the world.

5th | United Kingdom

Her Majesty The Queen has delivered a special address amid the COVID–19 coronavirus pandemic.

In a pre–recorded message, Her Majesty said the U.K. 'will succeed' in its fight against the coronavirus pandemic but may have 'more still to endure'.

The Queen also thanked 'everyone on the NHS front line, as well as care workers and those carrying out essential roles, who selflessly continue their day–to–day duties outside the home in support of us all'. She thanked people for following the government's rules to stay at home and praised people for coming together to help others.

The Queen said;

'While we have faced challenges before, this one is different'.

'We should take comfort that while we may have more still to endure, better days will return: we will be with our friends again; we will be with our families again; we will meet again'.

Her Majesty, who is currently 93 years old, said that the public's 'painful sense of separation from their loved ones' caused by social distancing reminded her of the experience of child evacuees during the Second World War.

The rare address to the nation came as the number of people who have died in the U.K. after testing positive for COVID–19 nears 5,000. The message was broadcast on TV, radio and social media, and was just the fifth time the monarch has given a special address in her 68–year reign.

5th |United Kingdom

Prime Minister Boris Johnson has been admitted to hospital for tests, 10 days after testing positive for coronavirus.

A Downing Street spokeswoman said that Mr Johnson 'continues to have persistent symptoms of coronavirus', including a high temperature.

6th | United Kingdom

Boris Johnson has been moved to intensive care after his condition worsened, Downing Street has said. A spokesperson for Number 10 Downing Street said;

'Over the course of this afternoon, the condition of the Prime Minister has worsened and, on the advice of his medical team, he has been moved to the intensive care unit at the hospital'.

'The Prime Minister is receiving excellent care, and thanks all NHS staff for their hard work and dedication'.

It is understood that Mr Johnson moved to the ICU in St Thomas' Hospital in London around 7 pm.

Dominic Raab will deputise for him as necessary, including taking on any security and coronavirus planning decisions as needed, whilst Boris Johnson will officially remain Prime Minister. Unlike in many other countries, the United Kingdom has no formal way of Prime Ministers being replaced or succeeded in the event that they are incapacitated.

7th | United Kingdom

Foreign Secretary Dominic Raab has said he is 'confident' that Prime Minister Boris Johnson will 'pull–through' and make a recovery.

Boris Johnson has reportedly received oxygen support but has not needed the support of a ventilator at this time.

Tuesday's full Cabinet meeting was cancelled, and Dominic Raab is now deputising for the prime minister, including by leading the government's response to the pandemic.

Michael Gove, the chancellor of the Duchy of Lancaster, said earlier today that he was now self–isolating at home after a member of his family began to display mild symptoms of the virus.

U.S. President Donald Trump said that he wanted to 'help' treat Boris Johnson, and said he had asked 'leading companies' to 'contact London immediately' about solutions. During a press briefing, Mr Trump said; 'We'll see if we can be of help. We've contacted all of

Boris' doctors, and we'll see what is going to take place, but they are ready to go'. It is unclear what help the President wished to offer.

8th | United States

Bernie Sanders has ended his campaign for the 2020 Democratic nomination, exiting the race for the White House.

The 78–year–old Senator from Vermont is largely known for reshaping American politics with his youth–led movement for sweeping change.

Bernie Sanders spent most of his career as an independent, but ran for the Democratic nomination in the 2016 election, running Hillary Clinton close in a race that she was expected to easily claim. His style of left–wing social–democracy has seen a significant wave of young people support his campaign, with him able to inspire a section of the party that other Democratic politicians had not been able to since the days of Barack Obama's primary run in 2008.

Sanders' departure all but confirms that former vice president, Joe Biden, will be the Democratic presidential nominee to take on Donald Trump in November's U.S. presidential election.

Mr Sanders' announced his decision during an all–staff conference call on Wednesday morning (8th). He told his aides that this was not just a Presidential campaign, but a movement which they should be proud of – pushing the Democratic Party to the left on many issues and seeing a significant change in the United States' politics.

9th | United Kingdom

Prime Minister Boris Johnson has left intensive care and been moved to a lower dependency ward.

His condition is believed to have improved significantly, having received oxygen whilst in intensive care. He will continue to be closely monitored according to Downing Street, but it is reported that he is in 'good spirits'.

A number of leaders throughout the world had sent their support and best wishes following the news that the Prime Minister was out of intensive care, as well as Labour leader Keir Starmer, who wished the prime minister a 'speedy recovery'.

12th | United Kingdom

Boris Johnson has been discharged from hospital and is to continue his recovery at the prime minister's country residence, Chequers, Downing Street has said.

In a video posted on his Twitter account, the Prime Minister said there is 'no question' that the NHS saved his life.

> *'It's hard to find the words to express my debt', he said in the video. He also paid tribute to healthcare staff that have supported him over the past week, paying special thanks to two nurses – Jenny from New Zealand and Luis from Portugal, saying they had 'stood by my bedside for 48 hours when things could have gone either way'.*

Downing Street said, 'on the advice of his medical team, the Prime Minister will not be immediately returning to work'.

The prime minister also thanked Britons for complying with the government's lockdown measures over the sunny Easter weekend.

14th | United States

President Donald Trump threw accusations against media and news organisations during the daily White House COVID–19 news conference in what has been described by CNN's Jim Acosta as 'the biggest meltdown from a U.S. President' they had ever seen.

During the press conference, Mr Trump played a video produced by White House staff which included a montage of selected clips of – Republican – state governors praising him for his handling of the coronavirus pandemic.

The president used the press conference to highlight what he'd done 'right' amid the pandemic, saying 'We've done this right, we've really done this right, the problem is the press doesn't cover it'.

Over 587,000 cases of the coronavirus have been confirmed in the United States, and over 23,000 people have died in the U.S. after contracting the virus – a death toll amongst the highest in the world.

One reporter asked the President what he had done to stop the spread of the virus during February, only for Mr Trump to respond by saying 'You're a fake, you know you're a fake,' adding 'You're disgraceful, you're so disgraceful'.

The president also claimed that he has 'the ultimate authority' to force states to lift their shutdown orders, a worrying sign for many that he may attempt to unilaterally take action against states' responses to the pandemic.

14th | United States

The International Monetary Fund (IMF) has released a report stating that they expect a 3% contraction in the global economy as a result of the coronavirus pandemic. This would be the largest contraction since the Great Depression of the 1930s.

However, this is a baseline estimate, which is based on the assumption that the threat of the pandemic will fade in the second half of 2020, meaning that a more protracted health crisis could result in an even steeper decline in the global economic output.

The 3% scenario is significantly worse than in the 2008–09 financial crisis, however, the IMF has suggested that there will be a sharp recovery from the pandemic. They predict that there could be a 5.8% gain in the size of the global economy in 2021, with the reopening of many countries locked down, allowing for a U–shaped recovery.

It is believed that many of the underlying economic principles will remain strong provided that the pandemic does not last too long, meaning that there will be a quick recovery should the coronavirus be eradicated in the coming months.

15th | United Kingdom

99–year–old war veteran, Captain Tom Moore, set himself a target of raising £1,000 for the NHS by walking 100 lengths of his 25m garden in Bedfordshire before he turns 100 years old at the end of the month.

In just one week, Captain Moore has smashed his fundraising target, so far raising more than £12 million for NHS Charities Together.

Captain Moore's campaign page on JustGiving has received donations by more than 633,000 people. A tweet posted on the Captain's Twitter account on Thursday read;

> *'Thank you so much to everyone who made this morning*
> *the most amazing and wonderful experience'.*
> *@captaintommoore*

Mr Moore trained as a civil engineer before enlisting in the army for the Second World War. He rose to the position of captain and served in India and Burma.

The walk, which Mr Moore finished on Thursday morning, is raising money for NHS Charities Together, a collective group representing and supporting the work of the NHS' official charities. The charities primarily pay for the services that are not covered by the NHS at large, such as care packages for patients and staff, as well as covering parking costs, accommodation and other volunteer expenses.

Having smashed his target and completing 100 laps, it is understood that the Captain will continue walking around his garden as donations keep pouring in.

Speaking on BBC News on Wednesday, Captain Moore described it is as 'completely out of this world' after he found out that he had raised over £5 million.

15th | North Korea

The leader of the Democratic People's Republic of Korea (DPRK) – more commonly known as North Korea – may be dead.

According to media reports, the North Korean leader, Kim Jong Un, has not been seen in public since presiding over a meeting of the nation's Politburo on the 11th of April.

It is not unusual for the leader to often go weeks without being seen in public; however, the leader missed the annual observance of his grandfather Kim Il Sung's birthday. Kim Il Sung was the founder of the Kim dynasty that has ruled the country since the mid–20th century and Kim Jong Un's absence has led to speculation that he is either dead or incapacitated. Many have suggested that his sister, Kim Yo–jong, is now the nation's supreme leader.

There are mixed reports about the whereabouts of Kim Jong Un, with some suggesting that he was having heart surgery, or suffering from the coronavirus. Others suggested he had died in unknown circumstances.

The United States have said that they are watching the situation closely, as a power vacuum in the country could result in instability for the Korean peninsula.

19th | United Kingdom

According to an investigation by the Sunday Times, the U.K. government missed multiple opportunities to reduce the impact of the COVID–19 pandemic.

According to the investigation, serious warnings from scientists were ignored, and there was complacency in government in late January and February. The newspaper also said that Prime Minister Boris Johnson missed five of the government's COBRA meetings as the COVID–19 outbreak worsened.

The investigation claimed that the U.K. lost 'a crucial five weeks in the fight to tackle the dangerous threat of coronavirus despite being in a perilously poor state of preparation for a pandemic'.

In its report, the newspaper also claimed that preparations for a no–deal Brexit 'sucked all the blood out of pandemic planning'. It claims that the country's last rehearsal for a pandemic was in 2016, which found potential issues with a lack of PPE; however, recommendations to address such issues were never implemented.

The publishing of the investigation led to #BorisResign becoming the number one trend on Twitter.

Speaking to Sky News, Cabinet Office Minister Michael Gove defended the Prime Minister and said: 'The idea that the Prime Minister skipped meetings that were vital to our response to the coronavirus, I think is grotesque'.

However, in an interview on the BBC's Andrew Marr Show, Mr Gove confirmed that Mr Johnson had missed the meetings, saying 'most COBRA meetings don't have the Prime Minister attending them'. Mr Gove argued that COBRA meetings were 'led by the relevant secretary of state in the relevant area'.

19th | United Kingdom

Dogs are joining the fight against COVID–19, with it hoped that they could identify the smell of the coronavirus.

Dogs have already been working in various settings for years to sniff out cancers, Parkinson's disease and improvised explosive devices. A medical charity that has successfully trained dogs to detect malaria is now hoping that they can train dogs to identify the smell of COVID–19.

The Medical Detection Dogs charity is working with the London School of Hygiene and Tropical Medicine (LSHTM) and Durham University to explore the potential for dogs to reliably detect the virus. If initial trials are successful, there are plans to train six dogs. As part of the training, it is believed the dogs would be given coronavirus patients' face masks to sniff to see if the virus has a unique odour.

The Medical Detection Dogs charity has produced more than 12 peer–reviewed papers during their work training dogs and has described its approach as 'rigorously scientific'.

It is not expected that coronavirus tests will be replaced with poodles any time soon.

20th | United Kingdom

An urgent appeal has been issued in the U.K. for volunteers to participate in human trials of a potential COVID–19 vaccine.

Teams at both the University of Oxford and at Imperial College London are to each get at least another £20m of public money after making 'rapid progress' in the hunt for a COVID–19 vaccine, Health Secretary Matt Hancock said on Tuesday.

The University of Oxford is to begin trials on 'healthy volunteers' from Thursday. The vaccine being trialled by the University is called ChAdOx1 nCoV–19. The vaccine is made from a harmless chimpanzee virus that has been genetically engineered to include part of the COIVD–19 virus.

According to the university, researchers plan to recruit a total of 1,112 volunteers, and up to 561 of those will be vaccinated with ChAdOx1 nCoV–19. The other volunteers will be given a control vaccine which protects against meningitis and sepsis.

The vaccine trial will last around 6 months, with an optional visit one year after vaccination. It is hoped that results from the human trials could be available as soon as September.

The vaccine being developed by the University of Oxford is made up of a weakened version of a common cold virus called the adenovirus. The adenovirus, which has been taken from chimpanzees, has been genetically altered so that it can't replicate and grow in humans, according to the university. The virus has also been combined with genes that make proteins from the COVID–19 virus (SARS–CoV–2) called spike glycoprotein.

Early findings have shown that animals who are given the vaccine are able to produce neutralising antibodies against the coronavirus.

23rd | United States

President Donald Trump has come under fire for suggesting coronavirus might be treatable by injecting disinfectant into the body.

Doctors and medical experts have strongly warned against the unproven idea, saying it is irresponsible and dangerous and could kill people.

Speaking during a White House coronavirus task force briefing, the U.S. President also seemed to suggest exposing patients' bodies to UV lights in order to 'kill it'.

The comments came after an official presented the results of U.S. government research that had indicated that the COVID–19 virus appeared to weaken more quickly when exposed to sunlight and heat, and that bleach could kill the virus in saliva or respiratory fluids.

While disinfectants can kill viruses on surfaces, they don't work inside the body. Consuming or injecting disinfectant into the body risks poisoning and death.

According to the latest figures, over 50,000 people are confirmed to have died from COVID–19 in the United States, with nearly 16,000 people dying in New York to date.

24th | United Kingdom

The Transport Secretary has announced that drones will be trialled to deliver medical supplies.

Speaking at the daily Downing Street coronavirus press conference, Grant Shapps said that he had 'fast–tracked' the trials for deliveries by drone, with the first trials to begin next week to carry supplies to St Mary's hospital on the Isle of Wight.

The trials are part of wider plans which have seen thousands of volunteers and vehicles put on standby to help frontline responders as part of a new Transport Support Unit.

According to the latest figures, more than 143,000 people in the United Kingdom have tested positive for COVID–19 and over 19,500 over those who tested positive have since died in U.K. hospitals.

26th | United Kingdom

Prime Minister Boris Johnson is set to return to work for the new week after spending recovering from the coronavirus.

Mr Johnson has been recovering at the prime minister's country residence Chequers since being discharged from St Thomas' Hospital in London on the 12th of April.

26th | Hungary

Hungary's government looks likely to push through legislation that will end the legal recognition of transgender people in the country.

The new legislation could see gender defined as 'biological sex based on primary sex characteristics and chromosomes', thus making it impossible for people in the country to legally change their gender.

The plans for legislation were introduced into the country's Parliament while attention is focused on the coronavirus pandemic. Hungary's Prime Minister Viktor Orbán has recently attracted international criticism by adopting legislation that allows him to rule by decree indefinitely. Parliament is still sitting in the country at this time but is focusing on issues such as new transgender legislation, rather than the COVID–19 pandemic, which has so far led to over 270 deaths in the country.

The proposed legislation comes after the government has become increasingly hostile towards the LGBTQ+ people in recent years. It has been suggested that if passed, the legislation could be open to challenge in both the Hungarian Supreme Court and the European Court of Human Rights (ECHR).

The degree of legal recognition provided to transgender people varies widely around the world. Most countries in Europe give transgender people the right to change their first name at least, and most allow people to change their birth certificates. Some European countries recognise the right of transgender people to marry according to their post–operative sex, including the U.K., France, Germany, Italy, Spain, Sweden, Croatia and others.

27th | United States

The United States' Navy has seemingly confirmed the existence of UFO's; releasing three videos that showed unknown objects in the sky.

The videos, which were taken by the Navy and released by the Pentagon, were reportedly leaked in days prior, with them now being made public to clear up several conspiracy theories circulating about them.

Taken between 2007 and 2017, the objects are all currently classified as 'unidentified', meaning that they have inadvertently confirmed the existence of UFOs, sending conspiracy theorists and amateur scientists wild with excitement.

29th | United Kingdom

Prime Minister Boris Johnson and his fiancée Carrie Symonds have announced the birth of a baby boy.

The couple announced at the end of February this year that Ms Symonds was expecting a child and that they had become engaged.

Johnson only returned to work in Downing Street on Monday (26th), having spent time in intensive care battling the COVID–19 coronavirus. It is understood that the Prime Minister will not take part in today's Prime Minister's Questions in the House of Commons and that Dominic Raab will stand in his place.

Messages of congratulations have started to flow in. Health Secretary Matt Hancock tweeted, 'So thrilled for Boris and Carrie. Wonderful to have a moment of unalloyed joy!' while the Labour leader Sir Keir Starmer tweeted, 'Wonderful news. Many congratulations to Boris Johnson and Carrie Symonds'.

30th | United Kingdom

Prime Minister Boris Johnson has said that the U.K. is 'past the peak and on the downward slope' of the coronavirus pandemic.

Speaking from Downing Street, Mr Johnson thanked the public for their efforts so far during the outbreak, in the first time Mr Johnson had presented the daily press conference since March, due to him suffering from a severe case of the virus.

Mr Johnson said that next week he would be explaining a plan to get the economy moving and to get people safely back to work and school.

The prime minister also added that face coverings might be useful as part of a lockdown exit strategy. Face coverings have already been recommended in Scotland, while some countries have made the wearing of face masks mandatory in some settings, such as on public transport.

An increasing number of tests have been completed each day for COVID–19 and, Mr Johnson revealed that 81,611 tests were carried out in the most recent 24–hour period, The government has a target of completing 100,000 tests a day by Friday.

According to the latest figures from all U.K. settings, 26,771 people have died from the coronavirus.

30th | United States

President Donald Trump has claimed that he has seen evidence that the COVID–19 virus originated in a Wuhan laboratory – though failed to comment on what this evidence was, or where it came from.

Mr Trump said that he feels confident that the virus came from the Wuhan Institute of Virology, adding that U.S. authorities were looking into it.

The president has refused to say what information he has to suggest that his claim is correct..

The Wuhan Institute of Virology has dismissed the allegations .Since the start of the pandemic, a number of theories have been floated as to the origins of the Coronavirus, though the actual source remains somewhat of a mystery.

30th | Russia

Russian Prime Minister Mikhail Mishustin has gone to hospital after testing positive for coronavirus.

Speaking on a televised video meeting with Russian President Vladimir Putin, Mr Mishustin said;

'The tests I did for coronavirus came back positive.'

Mr Putin has thanked the prime minister for his work so far and said 'what's happening to you can happen to anyone'.

Mr Mishustin has only been in office as prime minister since the 16th of January, previously serving as the Director of the Federal Tax Service for nearly a decade. Mishustin was nominated to be prime minister by President Vladimir Putin on the 15th of January, after Dmitry Medvedev resigned, along with the rest of the government, on the same day.

The prime minister's press secretary has said that everyone who has had face–to–face contact with Mishustin in the past few weeks will be isolated and treated for the virus.

It is understood that Mishustin will continue some work from hospital, and that Deputy Prime Minister Andrei Belousov will stand–in his place where required.

Recent months have been underlined by reports that the coronavirus pandemic is far worse in Russia than in many other parts of the world. Putin has been criticised for not taking the virus seriously, with many around the world noting that nationalist leaders have been amongst the worst in dealing with the pandemic.

According to the latest figures, over 114,000 people have tested positive for the coronavirus in Russia, and over 1,100 people have died after contracting the virus.

MAY

1st | Russia

Russian Prime Minister Mikhail Mishustin has gone to hospital after testing positive for coronavirus.

Mr Mishustin has only been in office as prime minister since the 16th of January; he was nominated by President Vladimir Putin on the 15th of January, after Dmitry Medvedev resigned, along with the rest of the government, on the same day.

Recent months have been underlined by reports that the coronavirus pandemic is far worse in Russia than in many other parts of the world. Putin has been criticised for not taking the virus seriously, with many around the world noting that nationalist leaders have been amongst the worst in dealing with the pandemic.

According to the latest figures, over 114,000 people have tested positive for the coronavirus in Russia, and over 1,100 people have died after contracting the virus.

2nd | United States

As if a deadly pandemic was not enough to be dealing with, a wave of deadly 'murder' hornets has been plaguing the United States.

For the first time, the two–inch–long hornets – originating in Asia – have been found in Washington State on America's west coast. Although they typically avoid humans, the hornets can kill people with multiple stings, although they are primarily known for attacking and killing bees, during their 'slaughter phase' of the year.

Scientists are racing to eradicate the hornets before there is a further impact on the nation's domestic bee population – beekeepers have already been reporting gruesome massacres in their hives.

2nd | North Korea

Despite reports that he had died, North Korean leader Kim Jong Un has appeared in state photographs, the first time he has been seen in almost a month.

The reason for his disappearance is still unknown, and there are suggestions that he was temporarily incapacitated, but it now appears that the reports of his death were false.

This is not the first time that the 36–year–old dictator has been missing, but the length of his disappearance, and the international turmoil during his disappearance were strange.

Some reports have suggested that the disappearance was due to Kim Jong Un recovering from heart surgery, although there is little evidence that this is the case. Others have suggested that he was potentially incapacitated due to Covid-19, after a number of other leaders have been left severely ill with the virus.

4th | United Kingdom

According to Downing Street, the NHS Nightingale Hospital in London is to be taken out of operation and put on standby, with no coronavirus patients expected to be admitted in the coming days.

The hospital in London's ExCeL Centre opened on 3 April with 500 beds in place and room for 3,500 more. The hospital took just 9 days to equip and fit, however, has received relatively few patients, as the existing hospital infrastructure has been able to cope with the increase in patients for the time being.

It is understood that the hospital could resume operations again if necessary.

Other NHS Nightingale hospitals have been built across the U.K. recently; however, reports have suggested generally low–usage of the facilities.

U.K. Prime Minister Boris Johnson announced last week that the country is past the peak of the virus. So far, 28,446 people are confirmed to have died in the U.K. from COVID–19.

5th | United Kingdom

We're 6 weeks into the coronavirus lockdown in the U.K., and as such, many people will be wondering what happens next. Lockdown can't last forever, and it seems that the next stage, whenever it begins, will involve the gradual easing of restrictions, continued social distancing and, crucially, contact tracing. One piece of technology being trialled to assist in this new stage is the NHS app.

The NHS contact–tracing app is expected to be rolled out over the coming weeks, starting with trials on the Isle of Wight this week. The app, which will be available for members of the public to voluntarily download on their smartphones, will let people know if they have been in close contact with someone who later reports that they have tested positive for COVID–19.

The app works using Bluetooth signals. In order for the app to work, you must have Bluetooth enabled. Questions have, of course, been raised about the security of the app and users' privacy.

Data from the app will not be linked to people's names but instead anonymous IDs. If someone is alerted that they have come into close contact with someone who now has the virus, they will not be told who that person is.

Users will be asked to share the first digits of their postcode, but GPS technologies are not currently used in the app to track people's whereabouts.

Other countries have also been rolling out similar apps to their citizens. The Australian government has launched an app called COVIDsafe in an effort to automate coronavirus contact tracing. In Singapore, an app called TraceTogether has been rolled out and downloaded over 800,000 times.

The NHS COVID–19 app is currently only available for use on the Isle of Wight as testing continues. If the app proves successful, it is expected to be rolled out to the rest of the U.K. within weeks.

6th | United States

The billionaire founder of car company Tesla, Elon Musk, has announced the birth of his first child. Musk and his girlfriend Grimes, announced that both mother and baby were doing well; however, people have been more interested in the child's name.

Elon Musk and Grimes have decided to name their baby X Æ A–12.

According to the pair, the unusual name will be pronounced as X–Ash A–twelve, with Æ being a ligature in Latin and old English, which is typically pronounced as Ash.

Writing on Twitter, Grimes explained their reasoning for the name;

'X – the unknown variable'

'Æ – my elven spelling of AI (love &/or Artificial Intelligence'

'A–12 – the precursor to SR–17 (our favourite aircraft). No weapons, no defenses, just speed. Great in battle but non–violent'

Grimes also said that the 'A' in 'A–12' also stood for Archangel, her favourite song – although nobody seems to know which song this is and who the artist is.

It is unclear whether the name will be legal, as names in California (where it is believed that baby X Æ 1–12 was born) must only contain the 26 letters of the alphabet.

The pronunciation of the full name remained somewhat unclear, but Elon Musk liked a tweet that asked whether it would be pronounced X Ash Archangel; perhaps this is how they will get around the pesky Californian law.

7th | United Kingdom

The U.K. government has said that some of the Personal Protective Equipment (PPE) that they ordered recently does not meet U.K. standards and won't be useable.

The PPE gowns – designed to protect the bodies of care staff – had been ordered last month, with 400,000 sourced from Turkey. They were not dispatched by the expected date, and the Royal Air Force (RAF) flew to collect them instead. However, it has emerged that of the 67,000 of those to have now arrived in the United Kingdom, 2,000 failed quality checks, and will therefore be unusable.

Currently, only 4,500 of the 400,000 ordered have been given to the NHS, although this is expected to rise.

A government spokesperson said that they were speaking to the supplier for replacement gowns or for refunds.

This comes after many complaints from NHS staff that they are being asked to work on the frontlines with inadequate, or in some cases, no, PPE, with worries about the virus impacting healthcare staff and causing infections.

It was reported last week that the government had asked individual NHS hospitals and trusts not to order their own PPE, but instead rely on the government's centralised procurement programme; this has been criticised due to the slow rollout of more suitable protective equipment.

8th | United Kingdom

The U.K. is marking the 75th anniversary of VE Day, although celebrations of the historic occasion will be muted due to the coronavirus pandemic.

On this day in 1945, Prime Minister Sir Winston Churchill announced that the war in Europe had come to an end after Nazi Germany unconditionally surrendered. The day has been named VE Day (Victory in Europe Day) and marked every year since.

This year's events to mark the historic day will be limited due to the lockdown. Events are still taking place throughout the day, but public gatherings have been cancelled. Many have been encouraged to have socially distanced street parties, with families having picnics on their own driveways.

The Prince of Wales and the Duchess of Cornwall will lead a two–minute silence at 11:00 BST to honour all servicemen and women during World War Two. A televised address is also expected from Her Majesty the Queen.

9th | India and China

There have been skirmishes on the border between India and China in recent days, with soldiers throwing stones at each other from both sides of the contested border around Pangong Lake.

It is estimated that around 200 soldiers were engaged in the fighting, that left several of them injured. For decades, the area has been disputed with frequent skirmishes occurring since the early 1960s when China launched a short, bloody, excursion into Indian territory.

Both sides stand by their claim to the territory. It is believed that recent skirmishes were provoked by Chinese soldiers, in response to India building infrastructure in the area, reportedly making it easier for troops to be quickly mobilised.

10th | United Kingdom

Prime Minister Boris Johnson has explained more details about a COVID Alerts System and how it will impact on social distancing restrictions.

The prime minister said that the U.K. is currently at 'Level 4' on the system and that we are now in a position to start gradually moving towards 'Level 3'.

On the system, Level 5 is the most severe level, while level 1 represents a time where COVID–19 is not known to be present in the U.K. The COVID Alert System was set out to the public for the first time at the weekend when Boris Johnson addressed the nation in a pre–recorded message, announcing the extension of lockdown measures but giving a roadmap for the gradual easing of some restrictions.

The COVID Alerts system may detect 'flare–ups' of the virus in certain areas of the U.K., with Boris Johnson saying that the U.K. would employ a 'whack–a–mole' approach to tackling these local outbreaks.

12th | Worldwide

There has been a significant increase in racially motivated violence towards Asian people as a result of the Covid-19 pandemic, according to recent reports.

One of the most shocking stories in the United Kingdom was the attack of a Singaporean student studying in London, when he was walking down Oxford Street. Jonathon Mok was set upon by a number of teenagers who were allegedly shouting 'coronavirus' at him. He was left with several injuries, with heavy bruising and facial bleeding.

However, this was not an isolated incident. Asian run businesses have been attacked and individuals have faced verbal abuse and physical assaults. Attacks similar to those reported in London have occurred across the world.

Two women attacked a group of Chinese students in Australia and the president of the United States has started using the moniker 'China virus', a not so subtle racially prejudiced attempt to deflect from America's poor virus response.

Countries throughout Europe, including Italy, who have been particularly hard hit by the pandemic, have reported around 50 racially motivated assaults against Asian people in recent months, whilst France and Russia have also been flagged by human rights watch.

The United Nations have recently stepped in, advising governments to take action to tackle the pandemic of racism that has proliferated in the wake of the virus pandemic.

13th | United Kingdom

The United Kingdom faces a 'significant recession' Chancellor Rishi Sunak has warned, with the economy facing its sharpest quarterly fall since the 2008 financial crisis.

Newly announced figures say that the economy has shrunk by 2% over the first quarter of 2020, with a sharp contraction of 5.8% in March. The 5.8% contraction is the steepest month–on–month fall since records began, despite the number only covering the first week of the lockdown, making a far steeper contraction likely in the subsequent weeks.

These new figures come just a day after Rishi Sunak announced an extension to the furlough scheme, with the government covering up to 80% of worker's wages through until October. It is expected that the extension of this scheme will help businesses across the country, many of whom may otherwise struggle to stay afloat during the crisis.

15th | United Kingdom

The jobs are 'gone for good'. In a tweet, former U.S. Presidential candidate Andrew Yang suggested that 42% of the jobs lost due to COVID–19 are not coming back. In the United States that equates to 15 million people who will likely struggle to get back into the jobs market after this crisis.

The situation is more complicated in the United Kingdom, with the furlough scheme put in place by the government largely keeping unemployment low and helping companies remain solvent. However, despite the extension of the scheme through until October, the long–term impact to the jobs market will be stark.

Economic crises often prove a catalyst for wholescale economic change; the 2008 financial crisis saw the loss of many manufacturing jobs that have since been outsourced or been replaced by automation. The trend is clear throughout history, the jobs market fundamentally realigns following major economic shocks.

Coronavirus is likely to cause a shift more stark than many previously seen, with many companies rapidly changing the way they operate in order to stay afloat, with these changes unlikely to simply snap back when the economy recovers.

Evidently the big winners of this crisis have been the online and technology companies, with Amazon taking on an estimated 175,000 workers during the crisis so far. Many brick and mortar businesses have equally seen their online presence surge, with the likes of Waterstones and WHSmith seeing a surge in online sales as their shops have remained closed – although have still suffered overall.

Without an ability to move online, even with government protection, the long–term viability of many companies is in jeopardy. The coronavirus pandemic is perhaps providing a disquieting foreshadow for brick–and–mortar shops, with the economic crisis likely to catalyse a shift online.

The workplace will also significantly change following the pandemic. Although most businesses currently plan to move staff back into offices after the pandemic, the ability for many service sector workers to work from home suggests a clear future in which this will become more commonplace.

The video–conferencing technologies such as Zoom and Google Meet have proven how successful remote working can be for teams, perhaps making it more likely that team members can work not just in different locations, but across different time zones and remain efficient.

Despite the coronavirus pandemic squeezing the jobs market, this means it could be younger workers who are set to benefit the most in the long term, with a higher take up of technology and online skills amongst this section of the workforce.

The hardest hit will indeed be the mid–career workers with a specific skill set that matches a job market that no longer exists, one that has been changed rapidly and beyond recognition into a futuristic online marketplace favouring those highly skilled in new technologies.

However, throughout the early months of the pandemic, it has been younger workers, and particularly young women who have been worst impacted. With hospitality and retail the most likely to suffer, areas with a disproportionately high female workforce, there are fears that the pandemic will only worsen the gender gap throughout the world.

We may only be months into the coronavirus pandemic, but its effects will change the economy and the jobs market beyond recognition. The world of work will be very different when we emerge weary–eyed from lockdown and stare into the reality of a new age.

15th | United Kingdom

Talks between the E.U. and the U.K. hang in the balance after U.K. chief negotiator launched a tirade against his E.U. counterpart, Michel Barnier, following the third round of post–Brexit talks.

Speaking following the latest talks, U.K. chief negotiator David Frost accused the E.U. of pursuing 'novel and unbalanced proposals' that would 'bind this country into E.U. law or standards'. Frost blasted the E.U.'s position as 'unprecedented in Free Trade Agreements and not envisaged in the Political Declaration'.

The comments suggest that the ongoing negotiations are proving difficult, with negotiators saying there has been 'very little progress towards an agreement on the most significant outstanding issues between us'.

The next round of talks will take place in June, but the current clear water between the U.K. and the E.U. over fishing arrangements is proving to be a significant sticking point for the future arrangement.

This comes against the backdrop of pressure within Westminster for the government to extend the transition period in order to ensure that a deal can be reached with the E.U. However, speaking in Parliament this week, Prime Minister Boris Johnson reaffirmed Britain's commitment not to extend the arrangement and the latest frustrated talks are unlikely to move that position.

18th | United Kingdom

Loss of smell and/or taste have been added to the U.K.'s official list of COVID–19 symptoms.

The symptoms join the list that had previously only included fevers and coughs.

Loss of smell or taste have been added following advice to the government from scientific advisers. Ear, nose and throat doctors have already been arguing for their inclusion on the list for many weeks.

The official lists of symptoms for the coronavirus vary by country, and some researchers believe that they are many more symptoms than are actually being announced by governments. The World Health Organization has said that along with symptoms of fever, cough and tiredness, people may also experience aches and pains, a sore throat, diarrhoea, headaches, skin rashes, conjunctivitis (red eye) and losses of taste and/or smell.

19th | United Kingdom

WWII veteran and NHS fundraiser Captain Tom Moore is to receive a knighthood, Downing Street has announced.

Captain Moore has truly captured the hearts of the nation over the last two months and has now raised around £33 million for the NHS during the coronavirus pandemic. Speaking following the news that he would become Sir Tom Moore, the 100–year–old said;

'I am absolutely overwhelmed. Never for one moment could I have imagined to be awarded with such a great honour'.

'I'd like to thank Her Majesty the Queen, the Prime Minister and the Great British public. I will remain at your service'.

Mr Moore also recorded a cover of You'll Never Walk Alone with Michael Ball, which went straight to number one in the iTunes chart. The version of the 1945 Rodgers and Hammerstein song, which also features the NHS Voices for Care Choir, has been raising money for the NHS alongside the Captain's walking appeal.

Prime Minister Boris Johnson recommended the award of a knighthood, which the Queen approved.

During the pandemic, many other people have also gone to special efforts to raise money for NHS Charities Together and other important efforts.

22nd | United Kingdom

Home Secretary Priti Patel has announced that quarantine measures will be imposed on new arrivals to the U.K. from 8 June, with fines for anyone breaching the measures.

Under the measures, people will be told to self–isolate on their arrival into the U.K., and anyone in England breaching the measures will face a fine of £1,000 or potential prosecution. Passengers will also be asked to fill in a form providing their contact and travel information so that they can be traced if COVID–19 infections arise. Anyone refusing to complete the 'contact locator form' will face a £100 fine.

A small number of people working in sectors such as road haulage and health will be exempt from the measures, as will people moving within the U.K.'s Common Travel Area with Ireland.

Arrivals into the U.K. will be asked to tell officials where they will be self–isolating. If the location does not meet 'necessary requirements', people will be required to self–isolate in government–arranged facilities. It is understood that the government plan for spot–checks to be carried out to ensure that people are self–isolating as per the guidelines.

Some countries have had similar quarantine measures in place since March, and some are now starting to ease some restrictions.

23rd | United Kingdom

The prime minister's chief adviser, Dominic Cummings, has defended making a 260–mile trip to be near relatives during the coronavirus lockdown, saying he did the 'right thing'.

Downing Street has said that Mr Cummings wanted to ensure he had childcare in case he got COVID–19 symptoms, though the Labour Party have said the explanation is not satisfactory.

Downing Street said in a statement;

'Owing to his wife being infected with suspected coronavirus and the high likelihood that he would himself become unwell, it was essential for Dominic Cummings to ensure his young child could be properly cared for'.

'His actions were in line with coronavirus guidelines'.

Mr Cummings has faced calls to resign over the trip, including from Ian Blackford, the Scottish National Party's Westminster leader. Scotland's former chief medical officer, Catherine Calderwood, and leading scientist Professor Neil Ferguson have previously resigned after breaking lockdown regulations.

Multiple members of the Cabinet have defended Mr Cummings' actions, including the Health Secretary Matt Hancock who tweeted;

'I know how ill coronavirus makes you. It was entirely right for Dom Cummings to find childcare for his toddler, when both he and his wife were getting ill'. @MattHancock

However, the tweet by the Health Secretary appears to go against official advice, which states that you should not leave home for any reason if you or someone you live with has symptoms of the coronavirus.

The trip was at the end of the March, at a time when the government was advising against all but essential travel. According to reports in a joint investigation by The Guardian and The Mirror, police in Durham spoke to Mr Cummings about breaching lockdown rules.

24th | United Kingdom

Prime Minister Boris Johnson has said that plans for the reopening of primary schools for key year groups will go ahead as planned on the 1st of June.

The prime minister acknowledged that not all schools may be able to reopen from the 1st and that reopening schools would be 'tough', but said that the government would continue to work with the sector moving forward.

Mr Johnson said that secondary schools should start to provide face–to–face contact for students in Years 10 & 12 from 15th June.

The announcement comes after concerns have been raised by teachers, doctors, and unions about the reopening of schools. The reopening of schools from the 1st of June is still subject to the government's five tests being met by Thursday (28th May), including there being evidence of continually falling death rates from the coronavirus in the U.K. The first minister of Scotland, Nicola Sturgeon, has tweeted a reminder that the comments on schools by the Prime Minister only apply in England.

24th | United Kingdom

Someone with access to the U.K. Civil Service Twitter account has tweeted their outrage at Dominic Cummings' trip to Durham, presumably before tendering their resignation.

> *'Arrogant and offensive. Can you imagine having to work with these truth twisters?' @UKCivilService*

The Civil Service implements the policy of the government and delivers public services; it is supposed to be a politically neutral body. The tweet was deleted within ten minutes of it being posted and the Cabinet Office later announced it was investigating the matter.

25th | United Kingdom

The prime minister's chief adviser Dominic Cummings has said he believed he was acting 'reasonably', as he explained his actions during the coronavirus lockdown.

In an unprecedented press conference in the Downing Street 'Rose' Garden, Mr Cummings explained his movements and actions during the coronavirus lockdown as a row has erupted in recent days, with media reports suggesting that he broke lockdown regulations by visiting Durham on two occasions.

Speaking on Bank Holiday Monday, Mr Cummings said he had travelled to Durham once during the lockdown due to concerns about care for his child if both he and his partner became ill, but he had stayed in a vacant house roughly 50m away from his parent's house and did not come into contact with them at any time.

He said that after arriving in Durham, he became ill and followed the guidelines to self–isolate. His child also became ill and was taken to hospital by ambulance, accompanied by Mr Cummings' wife.

When his child was discharged from hospital, Mr Cummings drove to the hospital, did not leave his car, and picked up his child and wife, driving them back to the house they were staying in, he said.

He said that before returning to London, he sought medical advice which said it was safe for him to return to working in Downing Street. Before returning to London, he drove with his child and wife for 'roughly half an hour and ended up on the outskirts of Barnard Castle town'. There, he sat next to a river outside his car for about 15 minutes, before turning around and then heading back home. He said the purpose of the journey to Barnard Castle town was not for sightseeing but was a 'test ride' to see if he would be able to safely drive back to London, given some problems with his eyesight while he was ill with suspected, but unconfirmed, COVID–19.

Mr Cummings said he has not offered to resign and has not considered it. At least 20 Conservative MPs have called on the prime minister's chief adviser to resign in recent days, along with MPs from other parties, members of the media and members of the public. Mr Cummings also said, 'I don't regret what I did'. He did though say that he thought he perhaps should have made a public statement earlier.

In answering questions from the media, the adviser to the prime minister said he thought his behaviour in the 14–day isolation period he undertook was reasonable and he hoped people would agree that it was reasonable given the circumstances he faced. He said though that he understands that some people may think he should have acted differently, such as by informing the Prime Minister of his intentions to travel to Durham.

Mr Cummings has said 'it's up to the Prime Minister' as to whether he keeps his job.

25th | United Kingdom

All non–essential retail outlets will be allowed to reopen from the 15th of June, provided the government's five tests have been met, and outlets are 'COVID secure', Prime Minister Boris Johnson has announced.

Outdoor markets and car showrooms will be allowed to reopen from the 1st of June, also provided guidelines are met. Mr Johnson said that the U.K. has been making progress in tackling the coronavirus and that the 'R' number of the virus (infection rate) remains below 1.

It is understood that the measures will only apply in England, as the devolved administrations of the U.K. have previously said that their nations will not follow timelines set out by Downing Street for the easing of lockdown measures.

The reopening of retail outlets will see more of the economy start to return to operation. Some retail outlets have continued to provide delivery services during the pandemic, though non−essential outlets themselves have had their doors closed to the public since the 23rd of March.

The government has set out guidelines to help workplaces like shops, branches and stores to be 'COVID secure' when reopening. When shops reopen, it can be expected that there will be measures similar to those in supermarkets, with limited numbers of customers allowed in stores at any one time, increased cleaning and strict social distancing measures.

If the U.K. continues to make progress and the number of coronavirus deaths and infections continually falls, it is thought that some of the hospitality industry may be able to reopen in early July, in line with the government's roadmap out of lockdown measures. The number of daily deaths from the COVID−19 coronavirus in the U.K. has been falling continually in recent times.

27th | United Kingdom

The Health Secretary has announced that a new test and trace system will be launched tomorrow.

Despite the previous enthusiasm surrounding the NHS tracking app, the test and trace system will go live from tomorrow morning (28th May) minus the use of the app.

The system will see anybody who has been in contact with a COVID−positive person told to self−isolate for 14 days, even if they do not develop symptoms during this time.

The system is widely expected to allow for a return towards normality, with it hoped that cases of the disease can be isolated in an attempt to keep the R rate below 1; most recent estimates put the current R between 0.7 and 1.

Test and Trace will see all those testing positive for the coronavirus providing details of people they have been in contact with, with those people to then be contacted and asked to isolate for 14 days.

The scheme will rely on an army of 25,000 contact tracers which have been recruited to track down all of those who have been in contact with COVID–positive peoples. It is unclear as to whether the app – which has been trialled on the Isle of Wight – will still form a part of the tracing scheme at a later date.

28th | United States

Protests have erupted in the United States after George Floyd was killed by Minneapolis police.

46–year–old Floyd, an African American man, reportedly died in hospital shortly after being handcuffed and held to the ground by police officers.

Footage has emerged that shows Floyd handcuffed at the tail end of a police car, with a white officer leaning his knee against Floyd's neck. Floyd can be heard pleading with the officers that he could not breathe, whilst onlookers tried to warn the officers as Floyd visibly deteriorated.

Floyd was taken to hospital after he lost consciousness, with it later emerging that he had died in hospital.

All four officers involved in the incident have been fired from the Minneapolis police department, with growing calls for legal action to be taken against them.

His family described Floyd as a 'gentle giant', with the incident reminiscent of the death of Eric Garner in 2014 – who was suffocated to death by officers in New York, infamously crying out that he couldn't breathe.

A statement from the police department involved suggested that the officers were complying with ongoing investigations into Floyd's death but would not rush to any judgement in the face of growing public pressure. Since his death, protesters have gathered across the city, with tear gas reportedly fired into protesters.

28th | United Kingdom

Prime Minister Boris Johnson has announced that from Monday, groups of up to six people will be allowed to meet outside together in England.

When meeting, people from different households should remain two metres apart, the prime minister said. People will be allowed to meet in gardens and other outdoor spaces, but people should not be inside other people's homes unless it is to access their garden.

Previously, guidelines stated that only 1 person could meet 1 other person from another household outside, maintaining social distancing.

While the government has said significant progress has been made in tackling the coronavirus, they have said the changes to lockdown measures are 'cautious' changes. Boris Johnson said that different parts of the U.K. are moving at different speeds and we 'cannot and will not' throw away the gains made so far. He also reiterated that there may be local responses to the virus pandemic, re–emphasising the 'whack–a–mole' approach he recently described.

Boris Johnson said the changes to the lockdown 'mean friends and family can start to meet their loved ones'. The easing of lockdown measures announced on Thursday apply to England – they do not yet apply to the other devolved nations of the United Kingdom. The results from the review of lockdown measures in the other nations are yet to be announced.

37,837 people have died with COVID–19 in the U.K. so far.

29th | United States

President Donald Trump has announced that the United States will be 'terminating its relationship' with the World Health Organization (WHO).

Speaking at a press conference in the White House Rose Garden, Trump said that he will instead direct the funds to other organizations. He announced that he would sign a proclamation to redirect funds to U.S. universities, removing America from the world's most prominent global health organisation.

Trump suggested that it was part of a move to address what he considers to be bias towards China from the WHO. This comes after he had tweeted 'CHINA!', earlier in the day – his reasons for doing so are unclear.

The United States President has spent weeks railing against the WHO after he felt they acted too slowly in responding to the COVID–19 pandemic and had favoured China, misleading the world over the threat that the virus might have posed.

Trump claimed at the press conference that China had 'total control' over the WHO, whilst using the occasion to repeat his accusation that China was at fault for the virus.

By terminating its relationship with the WHO, the United States could significantly weaken the health organization as it is responding to COVID–19. The U.S. is the biggest single contributor to the Geneva–based organization, paying in around $450m.

The death toll in the United States is now at 100,000 – the highest recorded in the world – and is expected to rise, with the United States having a scattergun approach to lockdown and testing.

29ᵗʰ | United States

Protesters have been gathering in Louisville after an African American woman, Breonna Taylor, was shot and killed by police during the middle of the night, whilst police raided her home.

Taylor was killed in March; however, her killing received little media attention at the time. Since the death of George Floyd was captured on camera in recent days, protests throughout the country have heated up, with similar protests emerging in cities across the country as other recent killings have come to greater public attention.

Plain–clothed officers stormed Taylor's home at 00:40, whilst she was sleeping, as part of a drug dealing operation. The officers were investigating the alleged involvement of Jamarcus Glover and Adrian Walker in drug dealing within Louisville, obtaining a no–knock warrant.

It was believed that packages were received by the pair to Taylor's address, despite neither being resident at the address, where her boyfriend Kenneth Walker (no relation to Adrian Walker) was also staying on the night of her death. There does not appear to be any information to suggest that Taylor was indeed receiving packages.

Protests have been spreading throughout the United States, with solidarity protests being held throughout cities across the country, with George Floyd's killing serving as a catalyst for the re–emergence of the Black Lives Matter movement; a movement for social justice for African Americans that originally emerged in 2013, following the death of 13–year–old Trayvon Martin at the hands of police.

31ˢᵗ | United Kingdom

Labour MP Rosie Duffield has apologised and stood down from her role as an opposition whip after admitting to breaching lockdown measures.

According to a report by the Mail on Sunday, Ms Duffield met her partner for a five–hour walk at a time when he was still living with his then–wife. The walk is understood to have taken place during April, at a time when guidance prohibited people from meeting with anyone from outside of their own household.

JUNE

1st | Democratic Republic of the Congo

If one pandemic was not enough, the government of the Democratic Republic of the Congo (DRC) has announced that there is an outbreak of the Ebola virus in Mbandaka, Équateur Province.

The country has long been ravaged by Ebola, which has slowly been eradicated throughout the region after a significant 2014 outbreak saw a number of deaths throughout the world. The disease is significantly more deadly than coronavirus; however, it is less transmissible and is unlikely to spread rapidly.

There have been six reported cases in the area, the highest number since a 2018 outbreak in the same region. The DRC is currently dealing with the coronavirus pandemic, as well as the world's largest measles outbreak.

1st | United States

United States President Donald Trump has threatened to deploy the military across the country, to stop the protests and rioting that have ripped through America since the killing of unarmed black man George Floyd, at the hands of four Minnesota police officers.

Trump stated that he had called on the governors of all U.S. states to deploy the national guard and 'dominate the streets', and threatened that if they did not, he would deploy the military to 'solve the problem for them'.

Whilst speaking to the press, Trump specifically stated the need to protect second amendment rights, drawing criticism for stoking the tension in America and insinuating that individuals should use their weapons to put down protests themselves.

The police's response to recent protests has been heavily criticised for the use of excessive force, with videos going viral seeming to show news reporters being arrested and shot at with rubber bullets.

An independent autopsy found that Floyd, 44, had been killed by asphyxiation and Hennepin County, Minneapolis, concluded that his death was a homicide. This comes after one of the officers involved in the incident had been arrested and charged with third–degree murder – which implies negligence leading to accidental death.

The protests and riots transcend the killing of one man and have come to represent a reaction against a system that sometimes sees different criminal justice outcomes for African Americans, with the protesters calling for fundamental systemic change in order to redress the balance of the United States criminal justice system.

An unarmed African American protester, David McAtee, was killed in Louisville after the police and members of the National Guard opened fire on a crowd. The police stated that this was in response to being fired on by protesters, but this account is disputed by eyewitnesses.

2nd | United Kingdom

MPs voted by 261 votes to 163 votes on Tuesday to end the 'virtual Commons'. In order to vote, members had to form a socially–distanced queue across hundreds of metres of the Parliamentary estate.

Due to the risk of coronavirus transmission, the Speaker of the House of Commons Sir Lindsay Hoyle had ruled that voting by members filing through the division lobbies was no longer safe. Leader of the House, Jacob Rees–Mogg, had demanded an in–person vote regarding whether to end the virtual commons and bring sessions back to being in person.

Scenes of the MPs queuing spread on social media on Tuesday, with many referring to the scenes as the #ReesMoggConga.

Some have described the scrapping of virtual proceedings as 'discriminatory' against those unable to attend Parliament due to the coronavirus.

MPs that were shielding were unable to participate in proceedings. Leader of the House of Commons Jacob Rees–Mogg has said that the government will lay a motion to try and ensure that some virtual proceedings can continue for members of the House that are shielding and unable to return to Parliament for medical reasons.

4th | United Kingdom

The wearing of face coverings on public transport in England is to be made mandatory from the 15th of June.

According to Transport Secretary Grant Shapps, those who do not comply with the new rules can be stopped from travelling and passengers can be fined. There are to be exemptions to the rule for young children and people with some medical conditions.

The U.K. government had previously advised members of the public to wear face coverings in enclosed spaces where social distancing is not always possible.

Advice from different authorities on the use of face coverings during the coronavirus pandemic has been mixed. Some countries have already made the use of face masks mandatory in many areas of public life.

In the U.K., the public is being told to wear 'face coverings', keeping medical face masks reserved for staff in the health sectors.

The announcement came as nearly 40,000 people are confirmed to have died with COVID–19 in the U.K.

6th | United Kingdom

Protesters clashed with police in central London during Black Lives Matter demonstrations following George Floyd's death in the United States last month, and wider protests have also taken place in multiple U.K. cities to protest the continuing legacies of slavery and racial injustice that continue to impact black people in the United Kingdom.

The majority of protests in the U.K. were peaceful, though some turned violent with bottles, flares and other items thrown towards police and Downing Street. One officer was knocked from their horse during protests after colliding with a traffic light as police responded to protests outside Downing Street.

Many of the protesters have taken to social media to make it clear that they disagree with the actions of some other protesters. During the protests, a statue of Sir Winston Churchill in Parliament Square was defaced, on what is the 76th anniversary of the D–Day landings, with Churchill holding infamously racist views and having been accused of causing a famine in India and the massacres of Africans during the Boer War.

Thousands of people gathered in Parliament Square and nearby locations in London for protests; many of those in attendance were wearing face coverings and practicing social distancing. The previous day, Health Secretary Matt Hancock had urged people not to break lockdown rules for protests. Mr Hancock said;

'Like so many, I am appalled by the death of George Floyd and I understand why people are deeply upset, but we are still facing a health crisis and coronavirus remains a real threat'.

'So please, for the safety of your loved ones, do not attend large gatherings, including demonstrations of more than six people'.

Some of the signs being used by protesters said that racism was also a pandemic and a killer, one that deserves just as much, if not more, attention than the coronavirus itself.

7th | United Kingdom

A statue of former Bristol–born merchant has been torn down in the city during Black Lives Matter Protests.

Edward Colston, a former slave trader, had his statue brought down by protesters due to his entwinement with the legacies of slavery, with protesters dragging the statue towards the Bristol harbour and pushing it into the water.

The Home Secretary, Priti Patel, called the actions 'utterly disgraceful' and said that it detracted from the cause protesters were fighting for.

Others have been more sympathetic to protesters, considering it inappropriate to have such a statue in 21st century Britain, although have criticised the methods of protesters, instead calling for statues to be taken down as a result of a review. Protesters had been trying to have the statue removed for several years, however, Bristol City Council have reportedly been resistant.

Since the statue's dunking, thousands of 'statue defenders' have taken to the streets – particularly in London – to stand in front of statues and prevent them from being brought down or vandalised. This has led to many clashes between Black Lives Matters Protesters and the 'statue defenders' – many of whom are far–right activists that have been allegedly attempting to intimidate BLM protesters. There have been a number of clashes with police as they have tried to move the 'statue defenders' on, in an attempt to prevent any violence between the two groups of demonstrators.

10th | United Kingdom

Prime Minister Boris Johnson has said the government believes all five tests for easing lockdown measures are being met and has announced further adjustments to the lockdown.

Speaking from Downing Street, Mr Johnson announced;

— All shops in England will be able to reopen from Monday, provided they meet COVID–secure guidelines

— From the weekend, adults living alone in England and single parents with children under 18 will be able to form a 'support bubble' with one other household

— Outdoor attractions where people can remain in their cars such as safari parks and outdoor cinemas will be able to reopen from next week

— Zoos will be able to reopen outdoor facilities to the public from next week provided social distancing is maintained

— Places of worship will be able to open for individual worship from the weekend

The idea of 'support bubbles' is intended to help those facing social isolation during the current coronavirus lockdown – with many worried about the impact of the pandemic on mental health. Members of each bubble can visit and stay at each other's home without needing to social distance. People cannot be part of more than one 'support bubble', and those that are currently shielding cannot be part of any 'support bubble'.

16th | United Kingdom

The U.K. government is setting up a 'COVID Summer Food Fund' to help feed children during the summer holidays, it has been announced.

The announcement of the fund comes after Manchester United footballer Marcus Rashford called for a U–turn in government plans not to offer meal vouchers during the holidays.

The government would usually provide free school meals for some pupils during term time and had introduced a national voucher scheme for these students during the COVID–19 coronavirus pandemic when schools have been closed. However, the government had originally said the scheme would not be extended for the summer holidays.

Rashford has spent recent days urging politicians to ensure pupils can continue to access the voucher scheme during the summer, building a significant campaign through social media. In an open letter to MPs and in recent media interviews, the footballer has described his own experience of relying on food banks and often going hungry at school when growing up.

16th | United Kingdom

The Department for International Development (DfID) is set to be merged into the Foreign and Commonwealth Office, the prime minister has announced.

DfID has existed since 1997 and manages Britain's foreign aid budget, focusing on sustainable development overseas.

The announcement of the merger came as a shock to many, despite talk towards the end of 2019 suggesting that Boris Johnson planned to merge the department into the wider Foreign and Commonwealth Office in a bid to streamline the Civil Service.

Despite asserting that the government would maintain its target of 0.7% of GDP going towards foreign aid – a target first met under David Cameron's tenure as prime minister, the decision to merge the departments has been widely criticised.

David Cameron, Gordon Brown and Tony Blair have all criticised the move – three prime ministers who had the largest commitment to the department during their tenures, with the latter founding it in 1997. The Labour leader Sir Keir Starmer has said the merger 'diminishes Britain's place in the world'.

DfID had aimed to support the United Nations development goals with its commitment to 0.7% reflective of the UN target set. The department has consistently invested in aid projects abroad which have contributed to the fall of global poverty and have helped the advancement of many nations.

16th | India and China

At least 20 Indian soldiers have been killed during further skirmishes on the India–China border in the Himalayas.

The Indian army had initially said that three soldiers had been killed, with casualties on both sides, but it now appears that as many as 20 Indians have been killed.

There are increasing fears that the border disputes could result in more significant escalation.

17th | United Kingdom

Premier League football has returned to TV screens, after Project Restart has allowed the 2019–20 season to resume – minus the fans.

Crowd noise was imposed into the background of televised matches aiming to give the illusion of normality to sport once again.

The first game back was not without controversy, with what is believed to be the first–ever failure of goal–line technology seeing a Sheffield United goal not given against Aston Villa – the game finished a boring 0–0, not fitting for the return of Premier League action.

18th | United States

Donald Trump is set to host a rally in Tulsa, Oklahoma as part of his bid for re–election, but the decision to hold the rally around Juneteenth – an important day in African American history – has caused uproar as the Black Lives Matter protests continue to grip the United States.

On the 1st of January 1863, Abraham Lincoln signed the emancipation proclamation, a document that stated: 'all persons held as slaves [...] are, and henceforward shall be free'.

Yet the 1st of January is not celebrated as the day that slavery was ended in the United States, as for a further two years, many white enslavers in the south refused to give up free people, whom they still deemed as property. It was not for a further two years that the final enslaved African Americans were freed from a plantation in Texas, on 19th June 1865.

The day is one of the most momentous in the American calendar, and the decision for Trump to hold a rally on this day during the midst of the Black Lives Matter protests shows either a catastrophic lack of historical knowledge or contempt for African Americans. Trump has recently said that the original date for the rally was not chosen on purpose to be Juneteenth and has moved the rally to the 20th of June.

His decision to hold the rally in Tulsa, Oklahoma is equally controversial; a city steeped in the racism that has haunted American history. In 1921, Tulsa served as the centre of what was perhaps the worst race riot in American history.

In Tulsa, a thriving, self–contained African American community called Greenwood – often known as the 'black Wall Street' – was turned into a hotbed of violence. A young African American man was accused of assaulting a white woman, with the white population of Tulsa attacking the black community within the city, burning Greenwood to the ground.

History sought to whitewash the events of Tulsa, with the African Americans blamed for decades for the violence that erupted.

The decision for the President – who has often been accused of dog–whistle white supremacy – to hold the rally on this day, in this city, is not just deeply controversial but could appear as a deliberate and systematic attempt to attack the Black Lives Matter movement.

Many teenagers, using the platform TikTok, have attempted to protest the President's decision by buying tickets for the event, with some reports of people in the United Kingdom and Korea buying tickets to attend the rally, in an attempt to leave the President addressing an empty auditorium.

It has been reported that there were as many as 1 million ticket requests for the 19,000–capacity venue, with it expected that the vast majority of that demand was the result of teenage TikTok trolls.

23rd | United Kingdom

Boris Johnson has announced that multiple coronavirus restrictions in England will be eased from the 4th of July.

Places of worship will be able to reopen for services and weddings will be able to take place with a maximum of 30 guests who are social distancing from each other, retail and hospitality will also slowly reopen.

The prime minister has said that some settings will need to remain closed for now, including indoor gyms, swimming pools, spas, nightclubs and bowling alleys. Mr Johnson said that the government would work with the arts sector to help choirs, orchestras, and theatres resume performances as soon as possible. He added that the government would release guidance for reopening for each sector.

From July 4, the 2m rule in England will be reduced to 'one metre plus' where 2m is not possible. Two households of any size will be able to meet together in any setting, including inside each other's houses and people will be able to stay overnight. Meetings of multiple households indoors are not recommended.

The measures announced by Mr Johnson will only initially apply in England. The devolved governments of Scotland, Wales and Northern Ireland have been easing restrictions at different speeds, and generally more gradually than in England.

25th | United Kingdom

Shadow Education Secretary Rebecca Long–Bailey has been sacked by Labour Leader Sir Keir Starmer for sharing an article containing an 'anti–Semitic conspiracy theory'.

A spokesperson for the Labour leader said on Thursday;

> *'As leader of the Labour Party, Keir has been clear that restoring trust with the Jewish community is a number one priority. Anti–Semitism takes many different forms and it is important that we all are vigilant against it'.*

Ms Long–Bailey was appointed to the position of shadow education secretary in April after Sir Keir Starmer became Labour leader. The MP for Salford and Eccles had run against Starmer in the Labour leadership election to replace Jeremy Corbyn, coming in second with 27.6% of the vote.

Ms Long–Bailey has now become the first shadow Cabinet minister to be stood down during Starmer's time as leader.

The article she had shared on Twitter was an interview with the actress Maxine Peake which contained a claim that U.S. police learnt kneeling on people's necks 'from seminars with Israeli secret services'. Ms Long–Bailey had shared the tweet and said Peake was an 'absolute diamond'.

Following her sacking, Ms Long–Bailey tweeted saying 'in no way was my retweet an intention to endorse every part of that article'. She said the interview's 'main thrust was anger with the Conservative government's handling of the current emergency and a call for Labour Party unity'.

25th | United Kingdom

A major incident has been declared in England after warm weather led to thousands heading to the beaches, with social distancing being ignored.

The news comes as many restrictions have been lifted and many more will be removed on the 4th of July, but the lack of adherence to distancing advice is leading to fears that there will be a second wave and that the government may need to re–impose some restrictions.

The prime minister warned the public that the lack of distancing could result in another spike of infections, as well as more deaths throughout the country.

There are fears that coastal areas will be the most likely to suffer from a wave of infections once the country begins to re–open more of its businesses.

26th | United Kingdom

Scottish Police have said that six people are being treated in hospital, including a police officer, who is in a stable but critical condition, after a stabbing attack took place in Glasgow city centre.

The incident happened on West George Street in Glasgow in the early afternoon. Police Scotland have said the situation is contained and that there is no danger to the general public. The street is closed off, and police have asked members of the public to avoid the area.

A male suspect was shot by armed police at the scene of the incident and has died.

27th | Republic of Ireland

Michaél Martin has become the new Irish Taoiseach, replacing Leo Varadkar, after forming a historic coalition.

Martin, whose Fianna Fáil party gained the most seats in February's Dáil election, has formed a coalition with former Taoiseach, Varadkar's Fine Gael, as well as the Green Party. It is the first time that the two major parties have been in coalition together; one of the parties has spent every year since 1932 in power, with bitter fE.U.ds often highlighting the last century of history between them.

The coalition was approved in a special sitting, held in the Convention Centre of Dublin, to meet social distancing requirements.

Both Martin and the outgoing Taoiseach, Varadkar, praised the moment as an opportunity to build unity in the country.

29th | Iran

Iran has issued an arrest warrant for U.S. President Donald Trump over the killing of top Iranian General, Qasem Soleimani.

The General was killed back on the 3rd of January this year, following an airstrike that was authorised by U.S. President Donald Trump. Trump, along with 35 others – mostly top U.S. military officials

– have been charged with various terror and murder charges by an Iranian court, 6 months after the General was killed.

Prosecutor, Ali Alqasimehr, announced the charges on Monday, stating that they will still attempt to pursue Trump, even after his presidency ends.

Countries cannot be forced to extradite those indicted by foreign governments, meaning it is unlikely that Trump will ever be placed before an Iranian court. Still, the decision sparks an unprecedented move by Iran after it was initially expected they were to take little action against the United States over the killing of Soleimani.

30th | United Kingdom

Boris Johnson pledged £5 billion to invest in building projects in the United Kingdom, as he started unveiling his recovery plan to bring Britain out of the coronavirus induced economic catastrophe.

The investment will include schools, roads and hospitals, aiming to create jobs and provide long term growth. Speaking on his Snapchat (yes, Snapchat) account, Mr Johnson stated his intention to either build or rebuild 50 schools across the country, to create better learning environments for children in the United Kingdom.

Before any journalists made comparisons between Mr Johnson's' coronavirus recovery investment and the New Deal programme, that led America out of the Great Depression in the 1930s, Boris Johnson said: 'It sounds positively Rooseveltian', making it clear the kind of esteemed company he wishes his leadership to be seen within.

> *'We will build, build, build. Build back better, build back greener, build back faster, and to do that at the pace that this moment requires'.*

30th | United Kingdom

On day 99 of lockdown in England, Leicester has become the first 'mole' to be whacked for their rising Covid–19 cases.

The local lockdown means that they will not be able to reopen pubs, restaurants and hairdressers on 4th July, meaning that for them, the lockdown continues.

Leicester currently has 3x more cases than the city with the next highest number, with a significant spike in recent days. It is unknown the exact cause of this spike, but it is perhaps a sign of things to come, with many other areas potentially going into more localised lockdowns.

Health Secretary Matt Hancock said that the measures would be reviewed in two weeks.

JULY

1st | Hong Kong

Several months ago – with China threatening to tighten the strings on Hong Kong – the United Kingdom's foreign secretary, Dominic Raab, announced the potential offer of extended residency to Hong Kongers eligible for a British passport. Yesterday, he was forced to act.

As a former British territory, approximately three million Hong Kongers are eligible for the programme, which Dominic Raab announced following China's decision to pass a new security law, which aimed to prevent the protests that have ripped through the city–state in recent months.

The new security law has fundamentally changed the legal system in Hong Kong, introducing new protest–related crimes, with severe penalties, as China has attempted to knock down the protests by the Hong Kong people.

Protesters have spent years protesting against the growing influence of Beijing over Hong Kong, which has served as a semi–autonomous region since 1997, where Hong Kong ceased to be a British territory and instead became a special administrative region of China.

Protests began in March 2019 when the government tabled extradition legislation, which would allow extradition to nations with which Hong Kong did not have extradition agreements, including China and Taiwan. This led to concerns that Hong Kong would be increasingly subject to the laws of China, ignoring its special administrative status.

These protests saw violent clashes between police and the people, resulting in the bill eventually being dropped, although protests continued about more general fears that Hong Kong could be threatened by the influence of mainland China over their semi–autonomous status.

This new security law seems to be emblematic of the increasing overbearance of Beijing into Hong Kong, and the vague wording of the

89

bill has created fears that it could be used to subjugate any resistance by the people against further mainland Chinese influence.

Analysis of the law by NPC Observer, a team of legal experts from the United States and Hong Kong, identified that 'its criminal provisions are worded in such a broad manner as to encompass a swath of what has so far been considered protected speech'.

Article 29 states that anyone who conspires with foreigners to provoke 'hatred' of the Chinese government, or the authorities, could have committed a criminal offence, meaning that the law can be used to stifle almost any opposition within the region.

Just a day after the law was passed, the first arrests were made in Hong Kong using its powers, whilst journalists and civilians have been pictured being knocked down by water cannons on the streets – despite not appearing to pose any threat or violation of the new law.

The United Kingdom's foreign secretary Dominic Raab responded by announcing in Parliament a new citizenship pathway, to potentially as many as 3 million residents in Hong Kong – with a bespoke new immigration system that will allow eligible people to live and work in the United Kingdom, before attaining citizenship.

1st | Russia

A constitutional referendum in Russia has returned a victory for President Vladimir Putin, with the nation approving an amendment that will allow him to serve a further two terms.

The change, confirmed in what was largely thought to be a manipulated vote, means that Putin – previously restricted to serving two consecutive terms – can remain in power until 2036.

Putin previously served as president from 2000–2008, where he was forced to step down and assume the role of prime minister (although largely remained in power as the nation's de facto leader). He returned to the presidency in 2012 and subsequently increased the term limits for a president from four years to six. In 2024 he would be due to step down again, however, the new amendment means that he can serve for a further two terms – he would be 84 by the end of this term.

3rd | United Kingdom

The U.K. government announced their list of nations exempt from a two–week quarantine period if individuals are to travel from abroad.

The long–awaited list includes 59 destinations where holidaymakers will be able to travel to, and return without being required to isolate for two weeks, with the level of coronavirus cases determining the list.

That means the popular destinations of Greece, France and Spain will all be exempt from the list, as well as Italy – the initial hotspot for the virus in Europe – also being from the new quarantine measures.

These rules will take effect from the 10th of July, whilst the developed administrations of Scotland, Wales and Northern Ireland will make their own announcements in the coming days on restrictions within these nations in the coming days.

Although England will not quarantine people coming back into the country, this does not necessarily permit restrictions to be lifted upon arrival in certain destinations – with New Zealand suggesting they had no intention to lift the current isolation restrictions on Brits travelling to the country any time soon.

4th | United Kingdom

Thousands of pubs across England have re–opened on what is being dubbed 'Super Saturday', as many lockdown restrictions are ended.

The government announced last week that many businesses will re–open, however, not all pubs and bars that are eligible to re–open will be inviting customers back in. Only around 60% of businesses have reported that they plan to re–open today according to a report by the CGA Outlet Index.

It is not just local watering holes that are reopening, with hairdressers, restaurants and self–contained holiday accommodation amongst those also inviting custom back in.

The Coronavirus pandemic is by no means gone – the virus remains in England but lockdown measures have been eased to allow some return to pre–COVID normality.

The pandemic has had a detrimental impact on many parts of the hospitality industry, including pubs and restaurants. Some restaurants won't be opening their doors again – Las Iguanas, Bella Italia, Coast to Coast and Chiquito's are just some of the well–known restaurant chains that have announced closures to stores across the country.

Others have faced even more devastation, with Carluccio's amongst the high street brands that have gone into administration during the early months of the pandemic.

Businesses that are reopening need to comply with COVID–secure guidelines, such as ensuring the adherence to social distancing and strict hygiene measures.

7th | Brazil

Brazilian President Jair Bolsonaro has tested positive for coronavirus after experiencing a high temperature.

Whilst announcing the result of his test, Bolsonaro removed his face mask and continued to talk to a gathered crowd, with the Brazilian president known for his scepticism of the virus.

Bolsonaro had previously called the virus a 'little flu' and has been infamously sheepish to take any action. Brazil has amongst the highest infection rates and death tolls in the world.

Only the United States has had more recorded cases at this time, with the U.K. and U.S. the only nations with more deaths.

Bolsonaro has been accused of politicising the virus rather than taking it seriously and taking action to protect the Brazilian population.

8th | United Kingdom

Chancellor Rishi Sunak set out a 'Summer Statement' or 'Mini Budget' in the House of Commons on Wednesday; a scheme being dubbed 'Eat Out To Help Out' has drawn particular attention.

Opening his statement in Parliament, Mr Sunak said; 'People need to know that although hardship lies ahead, no one will be left without hope.'

The Chancellor announced a plan to help keep furloughed workers in their jobs when the Job Retention Scheme ends in October. Mr Sunak said the 'Job Retention Bonus' would see employers paid £1,000 for every furloughed employee they bring back to work and keep in their jobs until January 2021 (and provided certain conditions are met).

Sunak's major announcement, the 'Eat Out To Help Out' Scheme, drew particular attraction from Twitter users. The scheme will see customers given 50% discounts on eating out between Monday and Wednesday, with businesses able to reclaim the difference from the government.

14th | United Kingdom

The government have done a complete U–turn on their previous decision to permit Huawei to build parts of the countries 5G network, now stating that it will remove any 5G technology from the network by 2027.

The government were criticised in January for their decision to approve Huawei a significant role in building the U.K.'s 5G infrastructure, before reversing that decision in May.

They have now gone further and committed to removing any existing technology, following a review by the National Cyber Security Centre (NCSC).

There will be a total ban on any new Huawei 5G kits from 31st December 2020 onwards, and a weaning off of the existing Huawei technology.

It is believed that the decision was in response to U.S. sanctions imposed against Huawei.

15th | United Kingdom

Manchester United and England footballer Marcus Rashford is to receive an honorary doctorate from The University of Manchester in recognition of his campaign against child poverty and sporting achievements.

Rashford, 22, will be the youngest ever recipient of an honorary degree from The University of Manchester.

Last month, Marcus Rashford spent days urging politicians to ensure school pupils can continue to access meal vouchers during the summer. The footballer built a significant campaign on social media and in media interviews, describing his own past experience of relying on free school meals.

The government would usually provide free school meals for some pupils during term time and had introduced a national voucher scheme for these students during the COVID–19 coronavirus pandemic when schools have been closed. However, the government had originally said the scheme would not be extended for the summer holidays.

On the 16th of June, the government announced a U–turn, saying it was setting up a COVID Summer Food Fund, meaning children eligible for free school meals in term time in England will get a six–week voucher to use in the summer.

16th | United Kingdom

Julian Lewis – the new chair of the House of Commons Intelligence and Security Committee (ISC) – has hit out after being sacked as a Tory MP for defeating the government's choice to chair the committee.

Last night, the government removed the whip from Lewis, meaning that although still an MP, he is no longer part of the Conservative Parliamentary party.

This comes after Lewis worked with Labour MP's to defeat Chris Grayling – No. 10's pick to chair the committee – and won the position as chair of the committee.

Lewis has called out the government, saying that their move to install Grayling as chair of the committee was an 'improper request' and that he was perfectly entitled to run as committee chair.

It was alleged that the government wanted to install Grayling to prevent the release of the Russia report – a document that was completed in the run–up to the general election – with allegations that it could be damning on Russian interference in the U.K. democratic system; the report is now set to be released next week.

The publication of the report had been delayed from the end of last year with Jeremy Corbyn criticising Boris Johnson's failure to release it during the General Election campaign in 2019.

This is not the first time that Boris Johnson has purged the Conservative Party of those who do not toe the line, removing the whip from 21 Tory MP's – including senior figures such as Ken Clarke and David Gauke – who failed to back him on leaving a 'no deal' Brexit on the table during E.U. negotiations.

19th | Russia

Russia's ambassador to the U.K., Andrey Kelin has sought to dismiss claims that Russia interfered in U.K. elections and allegedly attempted to steal British research into a potential COVID–19 Coronavirus vaccine.

The U.K., U.S. and Canada all recently discovered hackers launching attacks against their Coronavirus vaccine development projects. According to reports, hackers have used custom malware and have attempted to exploit other vulnerabilities in software to attack pharmaceutical businesses and academic institutions.

It is believed that the attempted hacks were to try and steal intellectual property, data and general research information from vaccine development programs.

The U.K.'s National Cyber Security Centre, along with Canada's Communications Security Establishment has blamed the attacks on the Advanced Persistent Threat 29 (APT29) group. Also known as 'Cozy Bear', APT29 is a Russian hacker group. Previous hacking attempts, including on the Norwegian government and U.S. think tanks are alleged to have been carried out by Cozy Bear.

On Sunday, speaking on the BBC's Andrew Marr Show, Russia's ambassador to the U.K. Andrey Kelin said that he did not believe the allegations put forward and that it was 'impossible' to link hackers to any one country.

20th | United Kingdom

Foreign Secretary Dominic Raab has announced that the U.K. is suspending its extradition treaty with Hong Kong 'immediately and indefinitely'.

Speaking to MPs in the House of Commons on Monday (20th), the Foreign Secretary repeatedly stated that the U.K. wanted a positive relationship with China but said that the country had committed a 'serious violation' of its international obligations through the introduction of the new national security law in Hong Kong.

An extradition treaty usually helps to speed up the process of an extradition (where a person is delivered to the law enforcement of a country where they are accused or convicted of committing a crime). The U.K.'s suspension of its treaty follows similar actions taken by the U.S., Canada and Australia.

Mr Raab also announced that the U.K. will extend to Hong Kong the arms embargo that has been applied to mainland China since 1989.

20th | China

In recent days, footage emerged on social media showing what appeared to be blindfolded Uighur Muslims being placed on trains and allegedly transported to 're–education camps' within China's Xinjiang province.

Evidence of the treatment of the Uighur Muslims minority within the westernmost region of China has been known about for several years, with the existence of such camps emerging in 2017, after several years of alleged abuses against the population of China's largest semi–autonomous region.

Following the emergence of this footage, political commentator and campaigner Maajid Nawaz, promoted a petition, before going on a hunger strike until the petition reached the 100,000 signatures required for a debate to be held in Parliament; the petition has since surpassed 120,000 signatures and will be considered for Parliamentary debate.

Speaking in Parliament on Monday, Foreign Secretary Dominic Raab, raised the issue of the Uighur Muslims during a statement on China and Hong Kong, before being pressed further on the issue by Shadow Foreign Secretary, Lisa Nandy.

Chair of the Foreign Affairs Committee, Tom Tugendhat, pressed Raab to take more stringent action and work with the United Kingdom's global allies to ensure that the issue is addressed fully, and strongly, through a global effort.

Xinjiang has been an autonomous region of China since 1949 when the Communist Party took power under Mao Zedong, although it is often called East Turkestan by the Uighur people – they have continually claimed that it should be independent of China.

There has been a reported 84% drop in birth rates amongst Xinjiang's Uighur population over the last few years, thought to be as a direct result of the policies pursued by the Chinese Communist Party (CCP) towards the Uighur Muslims.

In addition to the drone footage, it has recently emerged that 13 tonnes of human hair – allegedly shaved from the heads of Uighurs for use as hair extensions – had been seized by United States customs officials in recent weeks, bringing echoes of the holocaust and only deepening the calls for the United Kingdom's government to take more stringent action against the CCP.

China's Communist Party have previously stated that the decision to place several million Uighurs in 're–education camps' is motivated by terrorism within the Xinjiang region, however, presented limited evidence as to the necessity of this action, whilst the forced removal of children from their parents and widespread forced sterilisation and birth control constitutes genocide under the United Nation's definition of genocide.

Although the technical definition of what is happening in Xinjiang perhaps does not seem important, the use of the term genocide would be a significant step amongst the international community and would likely result in far more significant and coordinated global efforts against the Chinese government.

Uighur people are a Turkic–speaking Muslim minority within China, who have a long history of being persecuted within the country. The current internment of these people brings echoes of the holocaust in the 1930s and 1940s, where Jewish people were forced into internment camps, before being killed en–masse by the Nazi state.

China's government insist that their internment of the Uighur people does not infringe on their human rights, claiming that they are vocational training centres; they have continually refused to allow journalists and foreign access to these camps. Leaked Chinese government data show that the vast majority of those held have not been charged with any crime, allegedly detained for actions such as attending Mosques or practising their religion.

The United States government believe that they have enough evidence against CCP officials to impose significant sanctions against China, with intelligence suggesting that up to two million people are currently being held in internment camps, with half a million children being removed from their parents and placed in state–run educational institutions – likely aimed at significant cultural genocide.

Whilst information of activities inside the camps is limited, reports suggest that there is rampant sexual abuse, whilst interned Uighur people are forced to pledge loyalty to the CCP and renounce their religion.

21st | United Kingdom

The long–awaited 'Russia Report' from Parliament's Intelligence and Security Committee (ISC) has been published.

The report was published on Tuesday morning (21st) following an extensive inquiry by the previous committee that found that the U.K. is 'one of Russia's top Western intelligence targets'.

In the report, it is said that 'Russian influence in the U.K. is the new normal' and that 'Successive governments have welcomed the oligarchs and their money with open arms, providing them with a means of recycling illicit finance through the London 'laundromat', and connections at the highest levels with access to U.K. companies and political figures'.

The Committee's report confirmed that Russia tried to influence the Scottish independence referendum in 2014. It said that there had also been allegations of misinformation, bots and trolls being used by Russia to influence the E.U. Referendum in 2016. The Committee said on Tuesday at a press conference launching the report that the impact of such interference, such as whether it changed how people voted, would be difficult or impossible to judge, but that 'no one in government knew if Russia interfered in or sought to influence the referendum because they did not want to know'.

21ˢᵗ | United Kingdom

Calls have grown for Delyn MP, Rob Roberts, to resign or face disciplinary action from the Conservative Party after it emerged that he had been sending inappropriate messages to a 21–year–old female intern.

Messages that have been circulating on social media show him inviting a young intern to 'fool around' with him.

Roberts had earlier admitted to asking out another young female employee, leading to her moving position within Parliament; he stated that he recognised his actions in this instance were 'inappropriate'.

MPs across the house have called for the Conservative Party to remove the whip from Roberts, citing the party's decision to remove the whip from Julian Lewis last week, for beating Chris Grayling in becoming chair of the Intelligence and Security Committee.

A Conservative Party spokesperson said;

> *'Our party takes all allegations extremely seriously and has safeguarding and complaints processes in place to investigate complaints made to it under the party's code of conduct'.*

However, there are concerns that the party are not taking the allegations seriously, with this not the first–time serious allegations have emerged against him.

Rob Roberts came out as gay earlier this year but, according to a BBC report, told the young woman that 'I might be gay but I enjoy… fun times'.

Speaking to the BBC, the former intern said;

> *'I had had one of the worst days ever, and then I messaged him saying I'm crying, I'm not okay – and his solution to that was to proposition me'.*

> *'I felt really vulnerable and I felt like I was being used to make him feel better about everything'.*

25ᵗʰ | United Kingdom

Indoor gyms and swimming pools have started reopening in England as Coronavirus restrictions are eased.

Indoor gyms began reopening in Northern Ireland two weeks ago – they remain closed in Wales and Scotland.

Face coverings aren't required in most gyms; however, social distancing means some equipment may have been moved and there may be fewer stations available for use than usual. Some leisure centres are requiring members of the public to book in advance before using their facilities – each facility is likely to have slightly different rules and measures in place.

Some venues will open over the coming weeks as part of a phased approach to reopening, however, there are fears that many venues could stay closed for the longer term – or even permanently.

27th | United Kingdom

The government website displaying cafés, pubs and restaurants taking part in the Eat Out To Help Out scheme has now launched.

Members of the public can check which food outlets are part of the scheme, which is offering 50% off food and non–alcoholic drinks every Monday, Tuesday and Wednesday in the month of August this summer.

The scheme was announced by the Chancellor Rishi Sunak earlier this month to help support the hospitality industry as it reopens following closures due to the COVID–19 coronavirus pandemic.

Everyone in the U.K., including children, will be able to use the discount at participating U.K. cafes, pubs and restaurants on every Monday, Tuesday and Wednesday in the month of August 2020. The discount can be used an unlimited number of times, though takeaway orders or alcoholic drinks will not be included in the scheme.

The discount is 50% off food and non–alcoholic drinks up to a maximum discount of £10 per person. Businesses that are part of the scheme will be able to claim back the discounted money from the government within 5 working days.

However, ahead of the scheme starting next week, concerns have been raised about the government's messaging.

The U.K. government recently unveiled a new obesity strategy, with evidence suggesting that those who are obese face a significantly higher risk from the coronavirus. As part of measures announced on Monday, large restaurants, cafés and takeaway with more than 250 employees will have to add calorie labels to the food they sell under new laws.

One of the aims of the Eat Out To Help Out scheme was to get more people back to restaurants following lockdown – however, the messaging of the two campaigns conflict.

It would seem the message is Eat Out To Help Out – but don't eat too much.

30th | United Kingdom

The U.K. Chief Medical Officers have released a joint statement announcing the extension of the self–isolation period in the U.K. for anyone with coronavirus symptoms.

From today, anyone in the U.K. with coronavirus symptoms must self–isolate for at least 10 days.

Previously, people were only asked to self-isolate for 7 days if they had symptoms of the virus.

The new advice from the U.K. Chief Medical Officers brings the U.K. in line with guidance that has been issued by the World Health Organization.

30th | United Kingdom

From midnight (Friday 31st July), separate households will be banned from meeting indoors in large parts of Northern England.

People from separate households in Greater Manchester, East Lancashire and parts of West Yorkshire will not be allowed to meet inside each other's houses or any indoor venue under the new rules.

The new rules represent a tightening of Coronavirus restrictions following news that the U.K. experienced its highest daily death toll from the COVID–19 Coronavirus for more than a month in the last recorded 24 hours of data.

The restrictions will cover Greater Manchester, as well as other northern cities such as Blackburn, Bradford, Burnley and other surrounding areas.

The new restrictions are concerning after a period in which the virus had appeared to be retreating across the country. The restrictions also show a localised approach to tackling the virus where outbreaks of it are severe.

AUGUST

1st | United Kingdom

A former Conservative Party minister and sitting MP has been arrested after being accused of a number of sexual offences. The individual is currently unnamed, but the police confirmed that the man was in his fifties.

The alleged victim reportedly said that the MP had assaulted her and raped her, leaving her so traumatised that she had to go to hospital. The alleged assaults took place between July 2019 and January 2020, with the woman reportedly being a member of staff within Parliament.

The MP was arrested last night and remains in custody.

4th | Lebanon

At least 50 people have been killed, and thousands have been injured in a major explosion in Beirut – it is expected that the number of casualties will rise.

A building in the Lebanese capital exploded, resulting in a shockwave that was felt across the city and beyond, including 180 miles away in Cyprus.

Local reports have said the explosion happened at a building containing highly explosive materials and the blast led to significant damage or complete devastation to many buildings in the local area.

According to reports, some hospitals have been overwhelmed by the number of injuries. Lebanon's prime minister has said that those who are responsible for the blast will 'pay the price'.

The cause of the blast is yet to be confirmed.

5th | United Kingdom

Douglas Ross has become the leader of the Scottish Conservative Party, replacing Jackson Carlaw.

Ross is a member of the Westminster Parliament for Moray, being first elected in 2017.

He is perhaps best known however, outside of Parliament, being a qualified football referee and often officiating games in Scotland whilst sitting as an MP.

He has acted as a linesman in two Scottish Cup finals, as well as being involved in officiating a number of Champions League and international fixtures.

9th | United Kingdom

A number of demonstrations have taken place in a number of U.K. cities over the weekend including in Brighton, London, Liverpool and Norwich, with people demonstrating against the use of Coronavirus testing, face masks, lockdowns, vaccines and other Coronavirus related measures.

Demonstrations by anti–vaccine movements are not exactly new, though appear to have been growing in voice in the U.K. recently. Similar demonstrations have also taken place in the United States.

Some protestors have been claiming that masks don't work, are bad for health and are a violation of their personal freedoms. Similar claims are made about vaccines by anti–vaccine movements, members of which often refuse to take vaccines for religious or political reasons or because they consider them to not work. There are currently no coronavirus vaccines available in the U.K., though vaccines are considered the way out of virus restrictions.

The demonstrations in the U.K. have been generally been fairly small in size, however, could spark concerns in governments which are trying to enforce coronavirus restrictions.

10th | Lebanon

The explosion in Beruit on the 4th of August is now thought to have killed around 160 people, and recent days have also seen the resignation of the entire government. The world's attention has turned towards what has been a steadily growing humanitarian crisis in the country.

Yesterday, the prime minister of Lebanon, Hassan Diab, resigned after more than a third of his Cabinet also decided to step down from the government, just six months after taking office. This follows rising inflation – particularly on food – and widespread corruption within the country, which Diab lambasted as 'bigger than the state' during a resignation speech on Monday night (10th).

Seven members of Parliament have also resigned, with a reported attempt to force further resignations and prompt elections in the country, potentially paving way for a government that could tackle the 'deep corruption' that runs through the country.

The situation in Lebanon has deteriorated quickly following the explosion at a port in Beirut, however, protests and tension have been rising in the country throughout the year. Ravaged by coronavirus, the nation has faced humanitarian crises which were only exacerbated by the deadly blast.

Aid organisations, such as the United Nations Food Programme, have been attempting to establish supply chains to ensure that Lebanese people are able to access food, with inflated food prices meaning that many people are unable to access nutrition.

Protesters have been gathering in Lebanon's major cities following the blast, which is believed to be the result of a stockpile of poorly maintained chemicals that ignited, destroying much of the surrounding area and damaging swathes of Beirut.

In lieu of better healthcare infrastructure, Lebanon has been relying primarily upon international organisations, such as the Red Cross, who are the largest provider of ambulances services within the nation.

11th | Belarus

Following Belarusian President Aleksander Lukashenko claiming victory in the Presidential Election, protests have erupted on the nation's streets after accusations of vote–rigging and corruption.

Lukashenko, who has been in power since 1994, has long been considered 'Europe's last dictator' and won the election with 79.7% of the vote, defeating Svetlana Tikhhanovskaya, leading to calls of rigging, after reports of her winning many precincts throughout the country.

Tikhhanovskaya and her campaign team have declared victory based on results from 20 polling stations, urging the real results to be released in the coming days – after the official results showed her with just 7% of the vote – and calling on her supporters to take to the streets.

It is believed that at least one person has died in clashes between protesters and police, with the police putting down protests, often violently, drawing criticism from many western leaders.

U.K. foreign office minister, James Duddridge stated;

> 'The violence and the attempts by Belarusian authorities to suppress protests are completely unacceptable'.

President Xi of China and President Putin of Russia both congratulated Lukashenko on his re–election, whilst Russia's permanent representative to the UN, Dmitry Polyanskiy, speculated that the West were in some way responsible for, or orchestrating, the protests in Belarus.

Lukashenko appears unmoved by the protests, urging protesters to 'calm down' and telling parents to 'check where their [your] child is, so it won't hurt later'.

As of yet, there is limited public evidence to suggest that Lukashenko had indeed rigged the election, however, with limited access for foreign observers, it is perhaps unlikely that the result will ever be properly verified, however, with the intensity of protests rising, there is a belief amongst many Lukashenko opponents that this could be their opportunity to oust 'Europe's last dictator'.

11th | Russia

President Vladimir Putin has said that Russia has become the first country in the world to approve a vaccine against COVID–19.

Mr Putin announced the regulatory approval of a vaccine produced by the Gamaleya Institute in Moscow, with the President claiming that trials of the vaccine have shown it to be safe and effective.

Trials of the vaccine on humans have been ongoing for less than two months. Officials in Moscow have described the speed at which the vaccine has been approved as evidence of the country's scientific expertise, though concerns have been raised elsewhere that the relatively short amount of time taken to test the vaccine may mean that its safety and effectiveness cannot be guaranteed.

Speaking at a broadcast meeting, President Putin said;

> 'I know that it works quite effectively, forms strong immunity, and I repeat, it has passed all the needed checks'.

The approval of the vaccine comes ahead of the conclusion of larger trials of it, usually known as Phase III trials. These trials would usually be completed before a vaccine receives regulatory approval.

Russia has the fourth–highest number of recorded cases of the virus in the world and more than 15,000 are recorded to have died from the virus in the country.

11th | United Kingdom

Exam results for thousands of pupils in Scotland are to be upgraded after the Scottish government agreed to withdraw results that were downgraded by a controversial moderation process.

Exams in Scotland were cancelled this summer due to the COVID–19 c pandemic and results for students due to take exams were instead calculated based off teacher estimates, however, some results were moderated. Since SQA Results Day last week, there has been a massive backlash and outcry from pupils about the moderations which saw nearly 125,000 estimated results being downgraded.

Teachers submitted estimated grades for their pupils, however, the Scottish Qualifications Authority (SQA) then moderated 26.2% of these. Of those moderated, 93.1% of the grades were downgraded.

It has been claimed that pupils who lived in less affluent areas had their exam pass rates downgraded significantly more than pupils living in affluent areas.

The change in grades is expected to see higher pass rates for National 5, Higher and Advanced Higher qualifications, versus the rates that were achieved under the moderated grades.

Pupils in England will be hoping for a smoother results day when A–Level results are announced in two days' time, however, there are fears that a similar situation may occur as results have been calculated based on an algorithm that relies on a school's recent exam history, each pupil's past exam results and also estimated grades from teachers.

11th | United States

Kamala Harris has made history by becoming the first African American woman and first Indian American to appear on the ticket for a major party in the U.S. Presidential Election, being selected as Joe Biden's running mate for the 2020 election.

Harris – a Senator representing California – was amongst the favourites to become Biden's VP nominee, after he had announced he would pick a woman as his running mate at the last Democratic debate, back in March.

Biden had reportedly drawn a shortlist of candidates which included many prominent women, such as Tammy Duckworth, Elizabeth Warren, Stacey Abrams and Gretchen Whitmer.

A former prosecutor, Kamala Harris made her name in California, working to become the state's attorney general; serving from 2011 until 2017, when she took office as the junior Senator from California. Harris had originally been running for President herself, announcing her candidacy in February 2019, but withdrawing later that year, before any primary elections were held.

During the early Presidential debates, she had clashed with Biden after he said only one African American woman had ever been elected to serve in the Senate, despite Kamala Harris becoming the second when she took her seat in 2017.

Since withdrawing from the Presidential race, Harris has been considered amongst the favourites for the vice–Presidential nomination, with numerous reports suggesting that the Biden team had been in touch with her long before the primaries were over.

Harris has been vocal on police and criminal justice reform in the United States throughout her political career, and the decision to pick her as running mate is perhaps fuelled in part by the rising tension between African Americans and the police in recent months.

Following the murder of George Floyd by Minneapolis police officers, the Senator was seen at protests in Washington DC, as well as being vocal about the need for reform. As a passionate speaker, strong campaigner and a popular party figure, Harris is the perfect candidate to inject energy into the Biden campaign, which had seemingly lost its way and was seeing its polling lead narrow in recent days.

13th | United Kingdom

Students across the country have been opening their A–Level Results today and many have been finding out whether they have been accepted to university.

With exams cancelled this year due to the coronavirus pandemic, results were estimated based upon teachers grades, however, many were then changed through moderation, with a moderation algorithm looking at previous results of each student and their school as a whole. Overall, there has been an increase in the number of top grades awarded this year, however, many students and teachers have been left angry, upset and frustrated at the controversial moderation system.

36% of this year's entries in England were lowered by one grade compared to predicted grades submitted by teachers. 3% were lowered by two grades and some are reported to have been lowered even further.

For A–Levels, the number of people awarded A* grades, A* or A or A*– C grades were all up from 2019, with 78.4% of entries being awarded an A*–C grade.

Due to the challenges presented by the coronavirus pandemic, many students have been receiving their results online, such as through email. Some students have picked up their results in person at schools, though social distancing has meant that many of the usual results day events have been put on hold.

17th | United Kingdom

Exams regulator Ofqual has announced that GCSE, AS & A–Level results in England this year will now be changed to teacher predicted grades, in a significant U–turn.

The announcement follows days of frustration, anger and uproar across the country, including protests calling for Education Secretary Mr Williamson to resign.

In a statement, Chair of Ofqual Roger Taylor said;

> *'We recognise that while the approach we adopted attempted to achieve these goals we also appreciate that it has also caused real anguish and damaged public confidence. Expecting schools to submit appeals where grades were incorrect placed a burden on teachers when they need to be preparing for the new term and has created uncertainty and anxiety for students. For all of that, we are extremely sorry'.*

With concerns being raised about the moderation system even before results day, Education Secretary, Gavin Williamson, had said that where students had achieved higher grades in mock exams than in their results handed down from exam boards, they would be able to use this as the basis for an appeal. However, details about how this would work were not worked out until the week of results day itself, and details were not announced until two days after results day.

Just hours after the exams regulator Ofqual published a list of criteria that schools needed to have met for mock exam grades to be considered valid, the criteria and guidance was pulled, with Ofqual saying they were reviewing the policy.

The latest U–turn will relieve many students; though, for some, it is feared that the move will have come too late, with their Post–18 plans already changed and many universities having already filled their spaces.

17th | Mexico

Hugely popular beer brand, made by Mexican company Cerveceria Modelo – Corona – has been hit badly this year, for obvious reasons.

Meaning crown in Spanish, corona (the virus) was named due to the pathogen's appearance, with the beer brand namesake not coming into the mind of researchers when naming the disease.

However, despite the unfortunate coincidence leading to many reports that people were refusing to buy the beer, out of some misguided fear that the bottle contained the virus, Corona remains the most valuable beer brand in the world.

Despite the owner of Corona reportedly losing more than £200 million in revenue as a result of the namesake virus, the brand has bounced back quickly in the past few months and sales figures have been relatively unscathed.

20th | Russia

One of Vladimir Putin's fiercest critics, Alexei Navalny, has been poisoned in a suspected nerve agent attack.

Navalny fell ill during a flight from Tomsk to Moscow, and was hospitalised in Omsk, after the plane made an emergency landing. Video footage showed Navalny in severe pain, with flight crew rushing to try and help him.

It has been announced that he is being ventilated in hospital and was in a medically induced coma. It is suspected that a tea he was drinking prior to the flight was spiked with a nerve agent; similar to the poisoning of former KGB agent Alexander Litvinenko, who died in London after his tea was spiked with a radioactive material in 2006.

In the days before the poisoning, Navalny had expressed his support for the democratic protests in Belarus and stated that the protests currently gripping Belarus would soon find their way to Russia.

It is not the first time that Navalny has been a target, having been hospitalised in 2019, whilst imprisoned. He had damage to his eyes and skin, leading to a belief that it, too, was a nerve agent attack; his doctor said that it was the result of undetermined chemicals, that have still not been identified.

He has also been the subject of several other attacks, including a Zelyonka attack in 2017, where a green dye is thrown over an individual, and although does not cause lasting harm, is difficult to remove quickly. It is believed that the dye was laced with other substances during this, with Navalny stating that he lost 80% sight in his right eye following the attack.

21st | Belgium

The European Union's chief negotiator Michel Barnier has said that a post–Brexit trade deal between the UK and the EU now 'seems unlikely'.

Meanwhile, Mr Barnier's counterpart, UK Chief Negotiator David Frost has said that an agreement is 'still possible and it is still our goal' but that 'it is clear that it will not be easy to achieve'

The comments on Friday came following the conclusion of the seventh round of post–Brexit negotiations between the UK and EU. The negotiations came after a previous round in July concluded with Mr Frost saying that 'considerable gaps remain in the most difficult areas'.

The UK has been negotiating it's future relationship with the European Union since it formally left the bloc on January 31 this year. It is currently in a transition period where it can negotiate a deal with the EU. If an agreement is not reached, the UK will face a no–deal scenario as the transition period ends on the 31st of December this year – this would mean the UK would have to trade with the EU on World Trade Organization terms.

22nd | Germany

Two days after being poisoned, Alexei Navalny has been evacuated from the country and taken to Germany for special treatment.

Medical staff initially said that he was too unwell to travel, but have since allowed him to be transported in a plane, chartered by Cinema for Peace Foundation, with him now being treated in Berlin. Navalny remains in a coma at this time and in a critical condition, although he has been described as stable.

26th | United Kingdom

The United Kingdom's foreign secretary, Dominic Raab, has embarked on a trip for talks with Israeli Prime Minister, Benjamin Netanyahu and Palestinian leaders, hoping to progress peace talks in the region.

During his trip, Raab has been meeting with Israel's Benjamin Netanyahu and the Palestinian President, Mahmood Abbas; the meetings were set to advance peace discussions following Israel agreeing to halt further annexations of Palestinian territory earlier this month.

Israel also recently established diplomatic ties with the United Arab Emirates (UAE) earlier this month and Raab's visit was expected to mark a move towards further peace within the region.

Before his visit, Raab stated: 'Israel's suspension of annexation is an essential step towards a more peaceful Middle East'. Before going on to say;

'It is important to build on this new dynamic, and ultimately only the government of Israel and the Palestinian Authority can negotiate the two–state solution required to secure lasting peace'.

However, the trip by Britain's foreign secretary is expected to deliver little of what Raab had hoped for, with the two–day summit kicking off with reports of Israel's Prime Minister urging the U.K. government to end the pursuit of sanctions against Iran – the region's largest power – leading to fears that talks will be bogged down by wider regional issues.

Whilst the recent events in the region have created a window of opportunity to boost the peace protest – prompting Raab's trip – the peace talks between Israel and Palestine have seen many previous flashpoints before in which the process was expected to be given momentum.

These have largely come and gone in the past with little progress; the plan put forward by Donald Trump last year – in which Israel were permitted to annex much more Israeli territory – was met with disdain in Palestine and has made progress more difficult in its wake.

It has been widely viewed that the United Kingdom carry significantly more diplomatic weight to encourage negotiations between Israel and Palestine following this move by Donald Trump, which has seen increased suspicion of the United States in recent months.

With decades of history behind the conflict, with Palestinians fighting for territory to be recognised along the lines of the 1967 partition – recent years have seen solutions proposed with significantly less territory ceded to a Palestinian state, leading to significantly less diplomatic resolve by Palestinian leaders.

It is also widely thought that Raab's background (his father was a Jewish refugee who fled Czechoslovakia for the U.K. in 1938) could add new impetus to the negotiations within the region.

Although there is renewed hope for progress in the region, the chance of Dominic Raab's visit making significant inroads in the discussions is yet to be seen.

27th | United Kingdom

Sir Ed Davey – the Member of Parliament for Kingston and Surbiton – has been elected as leader of the Liberal Democrats.

Ed Davey faced off against Layla Moran for the leadership following the departure of Jo Swinson, who led the party to a disastrous result in the December 2019 General Election, losing her own East Dunbartonshire seat. The final result saw Davey gain 63.5% of the vote to Moran's 36.5%.

Heading into the race as the favourite, Ed Davey garnered criticism for his role in the coalition government between 2010 and 2015, serving as the Secretary of State for Energy until he lost his seat at the 2015 General Election.

Returned to Parliament in 2017, Davey has been one of the most prominent figures in the party for years, expected to track a typically centrist path for the party, with the electorate being increasingly divided by Boris Johnson's leadership of the Conservative Party.

Having served as the interim leader since Jo Swinson's departure, Ed Davey was considered the more experienced choice and promised a 'national listening project' in an email to members following his victory, promising to make the Liberal Democrats 'relevant again'.

Davey is considered a pragmatic choice by the party, who wanted to shift away from a disastrous series of election results since the coalition government, seeing them slip back to be only the fourth largest party in Parliament – behind the Scottish National Party.

Defeated candidate Layla Moran congratulated Mr Davey on Twitter, stating;

'I look forward to working with him to campaign for a better future for Britain'.

28th | Japan

Japanese Prime Minister Shinzo Abe has announced his resignation as the nation's leader.

Abe is a long–time sufferer of ulcerative colitis, and a relapse of the condition in July 2020 has reportedly led to his decision to step down. He said that he would be unable to carry out his duties as Prime Minister whilst seeking treatment for the condition. He has stated that he will remain in office until his party finds a successor, with the Prime Minister refusing to endorse any potential candidates.

Abe was first elected as Prime Minister in 2006, serving until 2007 when his unpopularity led to his resignation. His Liberal Democratic Party subsequently lost power, but assumed leadership of the party again in 2012. He was then elected as Prime Minister for the second time in December 2012, going on to win re–election twice.

31st | United Kingdom

The last meals discounted through the U.K. government's Eat Out To Help Out scheme are being served this evening as the month of August draws to a close.

The scheme has seen people across the country enjoy 50% off their bill for food and soft drinks for sit–in meals every Monday – Wednesday during August (up to £10 discount per person per meal) in participating food outlets. Businesses that participated in the government's scheme by offering the discount have been able to claim back the discounted amounts, with around 84,000 outlets thought to have taken part. The latest data from the Treasury revealed that claims had been made for more than 64 million meals through the scheme.

Many restaurants were fully–booked at times, displaying the level of attraction added to eating out by the discount scheme.

Though many restaurants have seen sales at record or record–breaking levels during the scheme, restaurants and outlets in some locations have still struggled, with much of Britain's workforce still working from home and away from city centre offices.

Some members of the public are still apprehensive about eating out, with COVID–19 still in general circulation in the U.K. and the number of infections continuing to rise each day and many fearing that it will lead to a spike in cases.

To try and protect staff and customers from the virus, restaurants and cafes have had to comply with COVID–secure guidelines, including reducing the number of human contacts and in many cases, reducing seating capacity to better allow for social distancing. These measures, along with investing in safety equipment, have made it an even more challenging time for the sector financially after months of lockdown.

SEPTEMBER

Virus Cases Rise | New Restrictions Implemented

1st | United Kingdom

Marcus Rashford has formed a new taskforce, including some of the U.K.'s biggest supermarket brands to try and help tackle child food poverty in the U.K.

Rashford, 22, has written to every MP in the country to urge them to back his campaign, with him telling the U.K. government that 'the time for action is now'.

Some of the big names that are part of the footballer's new taskforce include Aldi, Asda, Co–op, Tesco, Sainsbury's, Waitrose, Iceland, Lidl, Deliveroo and the Food Foundation. The taskforce is calling for three policy recommendations to be funded and implemented by the government as soon as possible;

— Expanding free school meals to every child from a household on Universal Credit or equivalent
— Expanding holiday food and activities to support all children on free school meals
— Increasing the value of the Healthy Start vouchers from £3.10 to £4.25 per week and expanding it to all those on Universal Credit or equivalent

According to the taskforce, implementing all three policy recommendations would mark a 'unifying step to identifying a long–term solution to child poverty in the U.K.'.

The implementation of the recommendations from the National Food Strategy (commissioned by the government in 2019) would help to support over a million extra children and young people.

Over the coming days and weeks, it is expected that the Child Food Poverty Task Force will share stories on social media of children and their families going hungry.

4th | United Kingdom

'If he wants to know what misogyny looks like in modern Australia, he doesn't need a motion in the House of Representatives, he needs a mirror. That's what he needs'.

Those were the words of Julia Gillard in 2012, then Prime Minister of Australia, in response to the misogynistic past of Liberal Party leader, Tony Abbott.

Gillard's speech towards Abbott has hit the headlines again recently following reports that Tony Abbott was being considered – and now appointed – by the British government as ambassador for the Board of Trade.

Abbott was heavily criticised in recent days for his past statements in relation to women, but also on other remarks made towards LGBT+ people and supposed climate change denialism. Abbott has been a relatively vocal supporter of U.S. President, Donald Trump, also garnering criticism from many for his association with a President that has been known to make inflammatory, racist, homophobic and misogynistic remarks.

Tony Abbott had previously described abortion as 'the easy way out' and stated 'the housewives of Australia need to understand as they do the ironing'.

The former Australian Prime Minister, who succeeded Gillard in 2013, was a prominent opponent of same–sex marriage in Australia's 2017 referendum, whilst also describing climate change as 'faddish' and claimed the world was 'in the grip of a climate cult'.

The U.K. government have defended their decision to appoint Abbott to the trade role, expressing full confidence in Abbott's ability to serve, whilst the U.K. Prime Minister, Boris Johnson, also remarked that 'he did not agree with those sentiments', in relation to past comments by Abbott.

Leader of the U.K. Labour Party, Keir Starmer, stated that he would not have appointed Abbott for the role, whilst thousands have signed a petition stating that Abbott's views were disqualifying and urged Boris Johnson not to appoint Abbott.

Scottish Nationalist Party deputy leader, Kirsten Oswald, said the appointment was 'beyond indefensible', before stating: 'If holding misogynistic, homophobic, Trump–backing, climate–change–denying views, as well as saying that some elderly people with COVID–19 should be allowed to die, is what qualifies you for a role with this Tory government in promoting the U.K. internationally then it is not so much Global Britain as it is Little Britain'.

7th | United Kingdom

Prime Minister Boris Johnson is reportedly planning new legislation to override part of the Brexit Withdrawal Agreement.

It has been reported that the U.K. government is to publish a controversial section of the Internal Market Bill that is expected to 'eliminate the legal force of parts of the withdrawal agreement'.

The Internal Market Bill is intended to secure the 'seamless functioning' of trade between England, Wales, Scotland and Northern Ireland following the end of the transition period, but reports have claimed that the bill could effectively override parts of Withdrawal Agreement concerning the 'Northern Ireland protocol'.

Some politicians have warned that such a move could see U.K.–E.U. trade negotiations collapse and leave the U.K. headed for a 'no–deal' scenario at the end of the year.

The Withdrawal Agreement was a deal between the U.K. and E.U. that paved the way for the U.K.'s departure from the bloc on January 31, 2020. The U.K. is currently in a transition period until the end of the year, during which time it follows the rules set by the E.U. while discussions are ongoing over a future trade deal. Trade talks are set to continue this week, however, talks up to this point have seen multiple sticking points remain.

U.K. Prime Minister Boris Johnson has also set a deadline for trade negotiations to be completed. E.U. officials had stated that they wanted negotiations concluded by the end of October, but Boris Johnson has now said that if they cannot conclude negotiations by 15th October then the U.K. should 'move on'.

8th | United Kingdom

Social gatherings of more than 6 people are to be banned from next week, as the government responds to an increase in coronavirus cases.

Data reporting in recent days has shown the highest increase in coronavirus infections since May, with nearly 3000 cases reported daily.

The limit on gatherings was 30 people, however, from next week, this will be reduced to just 6. Number 10 has announced that the new guidance will apply to any gatherings, either indoors or outdoors, with a number of exceptions for sports, schools and businesses, provided they are COVID–secure. Support bubbles for vulnerable people, where more than 6 people are required, will also be allowed.

The new government rules can be enforced through £100 fines or through dispersal by the police.

9th | United Kingdom

Sian Berry and Jonathan Bartley have been re–elected as co–leaders of the Green Party.

Unlike other political parties in the U.K., the Green Party automatically hold a leadership election every two years.

Mr Bartley and Ms Berry won 49% of the first preference votes in the election, defeating Shahrar Ali and Rosi Sexton who ran as individuals in the election.

Meanwhile, Amelia Womack was re–elected deputy leader of the party – a position she has held since 2014. Bartley has been co–leader of the party since 2016, while Ms Berry has been co–leader since 2018, replacing Caroline Lucas who previously held the position. Lucas is currently the party's only MP, holding the Parliamentary seat for Brighton Pavilion.

Apart from its one seat in the U.K. Parliament, the Green Party plays a role in the administration of 18 councils. The party had around 50,000 members in 2019, during which year it won 2.7% of the vote in the General Election on December 12.

11th | United Kingdom

Coronavirus cases have been rising across many parts of the U.K. recently, with many of the new cases being attributed to young people. Some people have suggested a link between a rise in cases and the Eat Out To Help Out scheme run last month, in which the government encouraged people to head out to local eateries.

The rise in cases has led to multiple changes to coronavirus restrictions.

In Bolton, all hospitality outlets are now restricted to takeaway service only and venues required to close overnight between 10pm and 5am.

In Wales, localised restrictions have been implemented in the Caerphilly County Borough area. Among restrictions, people living in the area must remain in it unless they have a good reason to leave it and visitors should try to avoid the area wherever possible. Indoor gatherings between people from separate households should also be avoided and extended household arrangements have been suspended in the area.

In Scotland, tough restrictions on home visits now exist in much of the west of the country. People living in Glasgow, East and West Dunbartonshire, Renfrewshire and East Renfrewshire cannot meet other households in their homes, with the rules to also be extended to Lanarkshire.

In Birmingham, Sandwell and Solihull, households will be banned from mixing from next week and in Northern Ireland, new restrictions forbid people visiting other people's homes in most cases in a range of areas.

15th | United Kingdom

Last night (14th), the Internal Market Bill – a controversial piece of planned legislation that will potentially rip up parts of the E.U. Withdrawal Act – passed its second reading in the House of Commons.

The second reading is one of the primary stages for a bill to become law, with it now being sent to the committee stage where it will face greater scrutiny. The bill will then be reported back to the House of Commons chamber, where further opportunities for amendment and debate will be had, before a third vote that can approve the bill.

From there it will be sent to the House of Lords for scrutiny. If the bill passes all of the stages, it will then be signed into law as a statute by the Queen.

According to the government, the bill is designed to 'protect trade and jobs', in a post–Brexit Britain, however, it has received criticism as it is in contravention of the Northern Ireland protocol, which was a key element of the Withdrawal Act (which was the bill that allowed Britain's exit from the E.U. back in January).

Whilst the bill in itself does not break international law, it would allow ministers in the government the power to do so in the coming months and years, should they feel that existing legislation is incompatible with their aims.

Part of the bill states;

'Any other provision or rule of domestic law that is relevant international or domestic law ceases to have effect so far and for as long as it is incompatible or inconsistent with a provision mentioned [elsewhere in the bill]'.

This essentially states the bill can void any parts of certain legislation that the government does not like, which Conservative MP Brandon Lewis, in a statement to the House of Commons, admitted breached international law in a 'very specific and limited way'.

By overturning parts of the Withdrawal Act, the bill could be in contravention of international law.

Should this happen, it is expected to seriously damage trust in the United Kingdom's government, with countries such as the United States stating that they would not be able to do a trade deal with the U.K. should the Internal Markets Bill pass.

Although this is only the first stage of the bill, given Boris Johnson's sizeable majority, it is unlikely that the bill will be stopped from becoming law; even though 32 Tory MPs did not support the government in last night's vote (30 abstained and two voted against) it still passed by 77 votes.

One of the most significant amendments being proposed to the bill is that by Conservative chair of the Justice Select Committee, Bob Neill, which is set to be voted on next week. MPs urged the government to accept Neill's amendment rather than proceed with the bill.

The debate around the bill was highly publicised, particularly an exchange between the Prime Minister and Ed Miliband – the former Labour Party leader was standing in for current leader, Keir Starmer, who is self–isolating.

Miliband attacked Johnson for not knowing the contents of the bill, whilst calling out the Prime Minister as incompetent;

'What incompetence. What failure of governance. Boris Johnson can't blame Theresa May, he can't blame John Major, he can't blame judges, he can't blame civil servants, he can't sack the Cabinet Secretary again. There's only one person responsible – him!'

The bill, according to the government, is intended to protect the United Kingdom from being broken up by the E.U., with the Prime Minister defending the bill in an impassioned speech to the commons.

16th | Japan

Yoshihide Suga has become the new prime minister of Japan.

Suga was a long–time ally of outgoing prime minister, Shinzo Abe, and his humble roots (he comes from a family of strawberry farmers) sets him apart from the ruling elite that have traditionally governed Japan.

Suga spent his years after graduating from university in a number of junior political roles, working on political campaigns and later as a secretary to a Liberal Democratic Party (LDP) lawmaker. In 1996, he was elected to Japan's National Diet (Parliament) for the first time, rising to become a minister in 2005; when Shinzo Abe rose to the leadership in 2006, he held a number of Cabinet positions, before Abe's resignation the following year.

Suga took the position of chief Cabinet secretary in 2012, upon Abe reassuming Japan's leadership, gaining a reputation as his right–hand man, often dealing with the complex bureaucracy, whilst Abe provided a more public face to the government. This did not mean that Suga was out of the limelight, holding twice–daily media briefings and gaining a reputation as a competent operator during his eight years in government.

His selection as Abe's successor was largely a forgone conclusion, with many of the party's senior and most prominent members pledging to back him, before he even announced his candidacy, on 2nd September. He made history on Monday the 14th of September, when he was selected to succeed Abe as leader of the LDP, becoming the first prime minister not belonging to a major party faction of a political dynasty within the country.

18th | United States

Donald Trump has never been the most popular President with young people, but his latest move – banning TikTok and WeChat – will only further sour his reputation amongst young Americans.

The decision has been made, arguably, as part of a wider international political game that has seen the United States increasingly challenge the Chinese Communist Party and their growing influence over the American economy; others believe it is a reaction to young people using the platform to troll the President in June.

From Sunday the 20th of September, both TikTok and WeChat are being removed from all U.S. app stores, as the State Department announced they were set to enforce an executive order from President Donald Trump.

The concern over the applications is that they collect significant amounts of data from individual users, which the United States government are concerned could be used by the Chinese government to wield influence in the U.S.

TikTok is owned by ByteDance, a Chinese company that has reported close ties to the Chinese Communist Party, meaning that there is a potentially significant ability for the Chinese government to access and potentially use the data of American citizens collected by TikTok. Academics Clive Hamilton and Mareike Ohlberg in their book, 'Hidden Hand', state that there is relatively little separation between Chinese companies and the Communist Party, meaning that they would potentially have significant influence over the company.

American corporation Oracle, have been working on a proposal with ByteDance that would have TikTok spun into a U.S. company with an all–American board and a security committee with members who have government security clearance, in an attempt to arrest fears that the app could pose a security risk to the United States. However, as this potential outcome is yet to happen, the app will be removed.

There had earlier been a proposal that would see TikTok bought by American company Microsoft, owned by billionaire businessman, Bill Gates; this proposal never came to fruition despite significant talk about a Microsoft buyout of TikTok being imminent.

According to many experts, the future of international security will rely on data security, with concerns that companies with such close ties to foreign governments could undermine national security and create significant threats. Although many other nations are continuing to permit the use of TikTok – undermining some of the security claims made by the United States – it is clear that there is significant fear about data security easing its way into national security policy.

It is also speculated that the move is being motivated by the ongoing trade war between the United States and China, with Donald Trump challenging the previous trade orthodoxy to challenge the perceived influence of the Chinese Communist Party over the American economy.

This is backed up by many experts challenging the assertion that TikTok's collection of user data poses any national security risk. Barack Obama's former Asia adviser, Evan Medeiros, said the Trump administration had 'never articulated the national security rationale for banning TikTok'.

The suggestion is that although data security is a major concern for national governments, the case of TikTok does not fit within this concern and is instead motivated by outside factors.

It has been suggested that trade or a personal distaste that Donald Trump has for the app following its use to 'troll' Trump, could be the real reason behind the ban.

Users of the app outside of the United States will not be impacted and it remains a possibility that a deal can be reached that makes TikTok palatable to the President; unless it is indeed that his personal feelings about being 'trolled' are the real reason behind the ban.

19th | United States

Ruth Bader Ginsburg, a social justice icon and giant of American politics has passed away at the age of 87. The second woman to be appointed to America's highest bench, few people in history have had such a substantial impact on shaping the political and legal world as the late Justice Ginsburg.

In 1956, she was one of just nine women (from a class of 500) accepted into Harvard Law School, where her professor infamously asked the female students how they could justify taking the place of a man.

Whilst at Harvard, she wrote for the Harvard Law Review, before transferring to Columbia (another prestigious law school) to complete her final year, after her husband took up a job in New York City; she went on to write for the Columbia Law Review too, becoming the first woman to write for both publications. Her transfer to Columbia was principally motivated by the childcare duties that she shouldered following the birth of her daughter – even the most influential women's rights advocate of her generation was burdened by the gendered responsibilities placed upon women.

Graduating top of her class, Ginsburg did not receive a single job offer from any law firm in New York: 'I struck out on three grounds: I was Jewish, a woman and a mother', she later said of law firms' refusal to hire her.

In 1972, she co–founded the Women's Rights Project at the American Civil Liberties Union (ACLU), before becoming the first female tenured professor at her old law school, Columbia. She later became the general counsel for the ACLU where she brought 6 sex–based discrimination cases before the Supreme Court – she won five. Often this was as the legal counsel for men in sex–discrimination cases, using the male perspective in front of a male bench to argue for the importance of equality between the sexes.

'Fight for the things that you care about, but do it in a way that will lead others to join you'.

During the presidency of Jimmy Carter, she was appointed to the United States Court of Appeals, for the District of Columbia (Washington D.C.) circuit and in 1993 Bill Clinton nominated her for the United States Supreme Court. Ginsburg was selected to replace Byron White at the recommendation of Clinton's Attorney–General, Janet Reto. She became the second woman to serve on the Supreme Court after Sandra Day O'Connor. Her early years were marked by her lifelong battle against discrimination against women within the law, convincing the court to strike down a male–only admissions policy in the United States vs Virginia. '[the policy] serves the state's sons, it makes no provision whatever for her daughters. That is not equal protection', she wrote in the court's majority opinion.

'Women belong in all places where decisions are being made. It shouldn't be that women are the exception'.

During her Supreme Court career, she was often the most liberal voice on the bench, writing an opinion against the Supreme Court's decision to strike down portions of the 1965 Voting Rights Act. Whilst also being one of the most significant justices in pushing the court to rule in favour of equal marriage in the 2013 Obergefell vs Hodges case.

In her later years, she became a hero as often the sole fighter against a Trump administration that sought to strike down much of her life's work. Her fight to prevent the Affordable Care Act (Obamacare) being declared unconstitutional, ensuring millions of vulnerable Americans kept their healthcare insurance, and to strike down Trump's 'Muslim' bans were symbolic of why she became an internet sensation, gaining her the nickname: 'Notorious RBG'.

Whilst her health was failing, her resolve was hardening, and she fought until the very end – often whilst undergoing treatment for cancer – in order to protect the most vulnerable Americans. Her life was underlined by personal experience of discrimination and arduous battles for equality, but few figures in American history have done so much to fight against a system that, despite many believing is now equal, still discriminates on the basis of sex, race, gender, religion and disability. In her name, the fight for justice and equality will go on.

'Real change, enduring change, happens one step at a time'.

21st | United Kingdom

Chief Scientific Officer Sir Patrick Valance and Chief Medical Officer Professor Chris Whitty have led the first coronavirus briefing from Downing Street in weeks, warning of the potential for the virus to 'move very fast'.

Showing a graph during the briefing, they warned that the current trajectory of the virus was troubling and that it could grow exponentially if the public are not vigilant against the virus over the coming months. He warned that there may be as many as 200 deaths per day within months.

'50,000 cases per day by mid–October'.

Speaking on immunity, Patrick Valance stated that although an increase in antibodies would improve the ability for most to resist the virus, this will diminish over time and that a large portion of the population is still at a high risk of contracting the virus and facing significant illness. He stated that immunity may be higher in cities and that the spread may be slightly slower in these areas, but that there is low immunity in the population that will not stop the spread of COVID–19.

Professor Chris Whitty talked through a chart that showed how increasing cases had started in specific geographic locations (such as Leicester) where local lockdowns were needed. However, he showed that cases were now rising across the United Kingdom and that this was not a local problem but 'a national one'. This raises the likelihood of another nationwide lockdown in the coming weeks if there is no evidence to suggest the spread is slowing

The pair both stated that the doubling rate (where coronavirus cases can be expected to double) is around seven days, stating that we have now 'turned a corner', but 'a bad one'. Whitty also stated that 'the seasons are against us' by stating that virus cases will likely increase significantly, like seasonal flu, throughout the winter months.

22nd | United Kingdom

In a statement to MPs in the House of Commons on Tuesday lunchtime (22nd), Prime Minister Boris Johnson announced new restrictions to tackle the coronavirus pandemic in England – including a curfew for pubs and other hospitality venues.

The new restrictions come as COVID–19 cases have been rising in many parts of the country, sparking fears of a 'second wave'. The restrictions were announced following a COBRA meeting chaired by the prime minister and attended by senior government officials from Scotland, Wales and Northern Ireland.

The new restrictions announced on Tuesday apply in England, but similar announcements are expected to be made shortly by the governments in the devolved administrations.

The Prime Minister announced the following new restrictions, saying that we should 'assume' they will remain in place six months;

— All pubs, restaurants and bars in England will have to close by 10pm each evening from 24 September.
— Hospitality outlets serving food and drink will be restricted by law to providing table service and takeaway services only.
— Anyone who can work from home should now do so
— Weddings will be restricted to 15 people only (down from 30).
— Plans to allow limited crowds to attend sporting events and business conferences have been suspended
— The rule of six has been extended to 'adult indoor team sports'.
— The requirement to wear a face–covering has been extended to staff in retail outlets, people in taxis and everyone using hospitality services when they are not seated at a table to eat/drink.

Mr Johnson stressed that the measures did not represent a return to a lockdown as seen earlier in the year, and that the government was not issuing a blanket 'stay at home' message.

23rd | United Kingdom

At the first–ever virtual Labour Party conference in the United Kingdom, Sir Keir Starmer made it clear that he is different to Jeremy Corbyn.

The conference, that was originally meant to be held in Liverpool, was cancelled and moved online in light of the coronavirus pandemic, but it has not stopped Keir Starmer making a pitch for national leadership, emphasising how the party is 'under new management'.

Starmer's major conference speech suggested that the Labour Party will not revert back to the policies of old, but usher in a new policy paradigm, perhaps with a platform containing brand new proposals such as Universal Basic Income that have gained increasing traction in recent years, but are yet to feature on a major party platform.

Sir Keir Starmer was criticised for his attempts to woo working–class voters, with an approach that favoured talking about patriotism and family values, a policy move that was abandoned by Jeremy Corbyn and has been largely blamed for the loss of the 'red wall' across the north of England – the fact that he gave his speech from an empty conference hall in Doncaster (part of the red wall) was a thinly veiled pitch to these voters. The Labour Party's Shadow Foreign Secretary, Lisa Nandy, talked of 'putting Britain first' in the future, something that was pitched clearly towards those voters who abandoned Labour for the Conservatives in 2019 over Brexit.

Although deemed an effective pitch to win back northern voters by some, it was also heavily criticised for verging into nationalist rhetoric and 'legitimising the nationalist narrative of the Tories'. rhetoric.

In another attack on Corbyn – with Starmer being determined to draw a line in the sand from the past four years – the Labour leader talked about the need to get serious about winning, directly addressing the criticism that Corbyn's Labour was happier acting as a pressure group from the opposition benches, rather than a government in waiting – this was one of the major reasons for their failure in the 2019 election, according to Ipsos Mori polling data.

In his speech, Starmer was also brutal in his attacks against the Prime Minister. He called Boris Johnson out for his 'serial incompetence' during leading Britain through the coronavirus pandemic and repeated the line he has frequently deployed that Boris Johnson is 'just not up to the job' of being Prime Minister.

It was also clear that Keir Starmer wanted to allay the fears about Labour being 'soft' on issues of national security, with Corbyn frequently being lambasted by the media and the public for his opposition to Britain's Trident Nuclear Deterrent.

> *'Never again will Labour go into an election not being trusted on national security, with your job, with your community and with your money. That's what being under new leadership means'.*

The conference also gave the opportunity to draw a line under Brexit with Starmer stating in his keynote speech that Labour would not be the party that 'kept banging on about Europe', perhaps an attack on the Liberal Democrats, who have only just abandoned their commitment to re–joining the E.U. in their party's platform.

24th | United Kingdom

The NHS COVID–19 app is launching in England and Wales today with the ability to notify people if they have been in close contact with someone who has tested positive for the coronavirus.

Described as 'a vital part of the NHS Test and Trace service in England, and the NHS Wales Test, Trace, Protect service', the app is available to download for free from the App Store and Google Play Store.

The app has a number of features including;

— Trace – the app will alert people if they've been near other app users recently for 15 minutes who have tested positive for COVID–19
— Alert – the app will tell people the coronavirus risk in their postcode area
— Check–in – app users will be able to scan NHS QR code posters at the entrances of some venues in order to register their details to help with potential contact tracing
— Symptoms – the app will help users check their symptoms and see if they need to order a test
— Test – the app will help users book a test and record their test result
— Isolate – the app will provide a self–isolation countdown and advice for those self–isolating

The launch of the app comes following technical problems with the first version of the app, developed earlier 2020. In May, a first version of the app was piloted on the Isle of Wight but was later abandoned due to the app not working effectively. The U.K. government then changed to a model developed by tech giants Apple and Google, which the app launched today uses.

During the year, some privacy concerns have been raised about potential contact tracing apps. In a section on the app's support website though, it is confirmed that the new NHS COVID–19 app cannot use your GPS location. The app also cannot be used to check if people are self–isolating, or be used by law enforcement for similar purposes.

27th | United States

According to a New York Times exposé, President Trump paid just $750 in income tax in 2016 – the year he won the presidency. He paid the same again in his first year in office.

Throughout the previous fifteen years, he only paid tax on five occasions; the president paid no income tax in ten years between 2001 and 2016.

The tax returns that Donald Trump had long fought to keep hidden – despite Presidential candidates typically making their returns public during campaigns (Hillary Clinton and Joe Biden both did so) – were obtained by the New York Times, who revealed the reasons the President likely wanted them hidden.

The low income tax paid by the President may be the headline, but his returns also show significant conflicts of interest, as well as potentially criminal behaviour in either inflating or deflating the value of his assets; inflating to leverage against loans, deflating to reduce his tax bill.

Trump is currently under an audit by the Inland Revenue Service (IRS) meaning that they are currently looking into tax returns to ensure that they comply with the law – the returns suggest that he could face a bill of up to $100 million after he took a significant tax refund of $72.9 million. His tax returns also showed that he was funnelling money to daughter Ivanka Trump for 'consulting fees', totalling almost $750,000, for her supposed consultation work for real estate projects in Hawaii and Vancouver, Canada.

Perhaps the biggest takeaways from the New York Times' exposé through is how much trouble Trump's businesses were in, and how he is using the presidency to profit – despite donating his $400,000 Presidential salary to charity.

The tax returns show that Donald Trump has reported losing $315 million on his golf courses since 2000 and has lost $55 million on his Washington D.C. hotel alone. These losses either underly a President who has used shady accounting tactics to avoid paying taxes, or a president – despite being elected due to his business credentials – that is losing hundreds of millions of dollars on his business ventures.

Much of these loses have been recovered by taking loans, and Trump reportedly owes more than $400 million, most of which is due for repayment in the coming years. The returns do not make clear how he will pay for this, meaning that he may end up having to sell–off some his property, such as Mar–a–Lago or his gold courses.

He has however, reportedly been able to use his status as President to increase the prices at his residences and charge far more for membership of the Mar–a–Lago club, with lobbyists and foreign governments renting accommodation at far above their usual price – allegedly in an attempt to influence the U.S. President.

30th | United States

Neither candidate on the debate stage last night (29th), at the first Biden–Trump head–to–head debate, was able to cover themselves in any glory. Joe Biden drew criticism for often stumbling over his words (the Democratic nominee suffers from a stammer) during scripted remarks on vague policy and Donald Trump looked like a stroppy teenager, interrupting Biden at every turn to interject with falsehoods.

In the hours after the debate, CNN's fact–checker in Chief, Daniel Dale, spoke of an 'avalanche of lying' from Trump; Biden was not immune to misstatements and falsehoods, but on the whole, tried to remain grounded on planet earth. For Donald Trump – with a death toll of more than 200,000 from coronavirus, a hypocritical nomination of a Supreme Court nominee (he has nominated Amy Coney Barrett to succeed Ruth Bader Ginsburg) and disastrous poll numbers – the facts are so damning against him that he has to create a new world of truth that he can inhabit. One that does not make him look like a failed President.

'Clearly this debate was an embarrassment for the United States', said CNN anchor Wolf Blitzer following the debate; there is not really any other way to look at it. At 74 years old, Donald Trump was the younger man on the Cleveland debate stage, but a fresh spray tan did not make him the more youthful candidate; he looked tired and incompetent, interrupting every time his classmate told the teacher the mean things they had done.

Biden's main objective for the night was to not mess up. He currently has a healthy lead in the majority of swing states and is on course for not just a popular vote victory (with the candidate winning the most votes in an election seemingly irrelevant in modern America) but an Electoral College one. He mostly achieved this, there were no major fumbles and by contrast to the man who inhabits the office he aspires to hold, he looked like he knew that on a debate stage you should look 'Presidential', even if he could not achieve it himself.

One of the best lines of the night came from Biden after Trump continued interrupting him whilst trying to answer a question on whether he would pack the Supreme Court in response to Trump nominating Amy Coney Barrett for Americas top bench. 'Will you shut up man', became perhaps the most endearing line – in close competition with Biden calling Trump a 'clown'. Biden said what most of us have been thinking for years and his line certainly won him the debate amongst some viewers.

The one time that viewers did not want Donald Trump to shut up was when he was asked to condemn white supremacists, but in typical Trumpian fashion, many words were spoken, yet nothing was said. When asked by debate host Chris Wallace whether he would condemn white supremacy Trump said 'sure [...] but I would say all of the violence I see is from the left–wing', before condemning Antifa (a left–wing protest group) instead and stating 'proud boys, stand back and stand by'. The Proud Boys are a male–only neofascist organisation that have been known to engage in violence and intimidate Democratic officeholders – primarily those of colour.

OCTOBER

1st | Belgium

The European Union has begun legal action against the U.K. due to the U.K. government refusing to remove sections from its controversial Internal Market Bill.

The E.U. had asked the U.K. to remove sections from the bill, which could allow the U.K. to override sections of the E.U. Withdrawal Agreement signed off between the U.K. and E.U. ahead of the U.K.'s departure from the E.U. The E.U. had given the government a deadline of Wednesday (30th November) to remove these sections – something which the U.K. government has not done.

The President of the European Commission, Ursula von der Leyen said;

> 'This draft bill is, by its very nature, a breach of the obligation of good faith laid down in the Withdrawal Agreement'.

The European Commission has decided to send a 'letter of formal notice' to the U.K. government, with the U.K. having until the end of November to respond to the union's concerns over the draft bill.

The 'letter of formal notice' is the first step in the legal proceedings. Exactly what may happen during the proceedings is uncertain and it is unknown when or how long a process in the courts may take to be completed if the proceedings escalate.

The legal proceedings could potentially sour the mood in negotiations, but for now, the negotiations for a post–Brexit trade deal are still continuing this week.

1st | United Kingdom

SNP MP Margaret Ferrier was criticised by the leader of the SNP, Nicola Sturgeon, after she travelled on a train despite a positive coronavirus test result; she also attended Parliament between being tested and receiving her positive result.

Margaret Ferrier took to Twitter this evening to apologise for her actions, after finding out that she had tested positive on Monday (28th September). During that time, she had travelled back to Westminster from her Scotland constituency on a train, potentially infecting other travellers.

It is also believed that she spoke in Parliament following her result, with the MP making a statement at 6:20 pm on Monday evening.

Many of her SNP colleagues have called on her to resign from Parliament.

She has had the whip removed by the SNP and is suspended by the party pending an investigation – this means that a number of MPs from the three largest parties have all had the whip removed, meaning that the party have removed them from the parliamentary group and they sit as independents.

2nd | United States

President Donald Trump has tested positive for coronavirus, along with First Lady Melania Trump; they will go into self–isolation.

The President announced the news via Twitter last night and it is believed that Hope Hicks, one of the President's top aides, likely passed the virus onto the President and First Lady; she had received a positive test result in recent days.

Hicks was seen boarding Marine One (the presidential helicopter) with the first family just a day before her positive test result.

'Hope Hicks, who has been working so hard without even taking a small break, has just tested positive for COVID–19. Terrible! The First Lady and I are waiting for our test results. In the meantime, we will begin our quarantine process,' Mr Trump tweeted two hours before announcing his own positive result.

> *'Tonight, @FLOTU.S. and I tested positive for COVID–19.*
> *We will begin our quarantine and recovery process*
> *immediately. We will get through this TOGETHER!'*
> *@RealDonaldTrump*

International leaders have been giving their support to the president, with Boris Johnson – who was in Intensive Care with coronavirus earlier in the year – tweeting his 'best wishes to President Trump and the First Lady'.

Trump's vice–president, Mike Pence, released a statement saying he was 'praying for [The Trump's] full and swift recovery'.

2nd | United States

President Trump has been taken to hospital with COVID–19 symptoms just hours after testing positive for the virus.

Mr Trump was transported to the Water Reed National Military Medical Centre. In a statement, a White House spokesperson said that the President had 'mild symptoms' of COVID–19 and that he 'remains in good spirits.

It was added that he was taken to the Medical Centre 'out of an abundance of caution' and he has received a cocktail of drugs. His age and obesity (his 2019 medical records showed him to weigh 243 pounds, making him obese for his height and age) would likely put him in a high–risk category.

The president is reported to have been experiencing fatigue, though it is understood he is still carrying out presidential work. Election campaign rival Joe Biden, who shared a debate stage with Trump on Tuesday (29th), has since tested negative for the virus.

Trump has joined a list of world leaders who have contracted the coronavirus. Among those to have previously tested positive for the virus include the U.K. Prime Minister Boris Johnson, the Russian Prime Minister Mikhail Mishustin and Brazil's President Jair Bolsonaro.

The President's positive test for COVID–19 could lead to a chaotic final month of the U.S. Presidential Election campaign, with polling day in just a month's time.

6th | United States

'Don't be afraid of COVID' was the message tweeted by U.S. President Donald Trump on Monday (6th) just hours before he was discharged from hospital.

There have been conflicting reports over the state of the President's health through the weekend, however, the President has said he is feeling 'really good'. In a tweet, President Trump said;

> *'I will be leaving the great Walter Reed Medical Center*
> *today at 6:30 P.M. Feeling really good! Don't be afraid of*
> *COVID. Don't let it dominate your life. We have developed,*

under the Trump Administration, some really great drugs &
knowledge. I feel better than I did 20 years ago!'
@RealDonaldTrump

In a later tweet, Mr Trump said 'Will be back on the Campaign Trail soon!!!' – with voting day for the U.S. election now less than a month away.

Whilst being treated at the Walter Reed Centre, the president was criticised for putting secret service staff at risk, doing a drive by for supporters outside of the hospital in the presidential vehicle, 'the beast'.

Telling Americans not to be afraid of the virus has led some to criticise the president, as almost 210,000 people have died from the virus so far in the United States.

6th | United Kingdom

Boris Johnson has laid out plans at the virtual Conservative Party Conference for how his government aims to 'Build Back Better' following the coronavirus pandemic.

Mr Johnson told the conference that he'd had 'more than enough of this disease', adding 'your government is working night and day to repel this virus and we will succeed just as this country has seen off every alien invader for the last thousand years and we will succeed by collective effort, by following the guidance'.

The prime minister set out multiple plans as part of his vision for the future, saying that 'after all we've been through, it isn't enough to just go back to normal'.

Key topics in Mr Johnson's speech included the health service, education and training, and also plans to invest into the 'green economy'.

During his speech, the Conservative leader described how he wanted to get back to a time where 'hairdressers no longer look like they are handling radioactive isotopes' and 'when we no longer have to greet each other by touching elbows as in some giant national version of the birdie dance'.

The prime minister said that he 'had to admit' that the reason he had 'such a nasty experience' of COVID–19 was that he had a very common underlying health condition – he was 'too fat'.

He said that before catching the virus, he had been 'superficially in the peak of health', however, that he was 'too fat' – he used this as an analogy to describe how the economy was in good shape ahead of the pandemic, but that some areas had key issues.

Johnson said that since catching the virus, he has lost 26 pounds, saying 'you can imagine that in bags of sugar', adding that he is 'going to continue that diet'.

7th | United Kingdom

Labour Leader Sir Keir Starmer has called on Prime Minister Boris Johnson to publish scientific evidence behind the 10pm closing time for pubs following images of punters pouring into the streets and leading to fears that it is worsening the pandemic.

Currently, coronavirus restrictions in place across England mean that pubs and restaurants have to close by 10pm each evening. It had been suggested that the rule could reduce the number of new coronavirus infections being spread, with some people known to visit several pubs during the space of an evening. However, many have warned that the rule is in fact 'counterproductive' and there have been scenes of large non–socially–distanced crowds on streets and public transport after the 10pm closing time since the rules came into force.

Starmer called on Mr Johnson to publish the scientific evidence ahead of a vote on the rule by MPs in the House of Commons next week. The prime minister largely avoided the question, instead suggesting that the Labour Party could not decide its position on whether it supported restrictions.

Beyond scepticism about the effectiveness of the rule, the rule has made the environment even more challenging for businesses in the hospitality sector, which have already been struggling greatly from the coronavirus lockdown.

Pub chain Greene King announced it is to cut 800 jobs and close more than 25 pubs, partly blaming tighter coronavirus restrictions and the conclusion of the Job Retention (furlough) Scheme. A number of the chain's restaurants are remaining closed for now, with hopes that they may be able to reopen in the future.

12th | United Kingdom

A new three–tier lockdown system has been announced in England as COVID–19 cases rise sharply in many parts of the country.

U.K. Prime Minister Boris Johnson addressed the nation after updating MPs in the House of Commons on the new rules, following a meeting of the emergency COBRA committee.

The prime minister announced that regions will be classified as being on 'medium', 'high' or 'very high' alert, and that the higher the level, the stricter the measures will be that are implemented.

It is expected that casinos and pubs may be among businesses that could be impacted by new restrictions.

15th | United Kingdom

From the weekend, London will be placed into tighter lockdown restrictions, under Tier 2 of the local lockdown system, Health Secretary Matt Hancock announced.

This is the second–highest level of restrictions that can be imposed throughout England – only applied when an area is considered a 'high alert' area, under the new three–tier lockdown plan. The main change that this will bring for Londoners is no household mixing, including in any enclosed public spaces, such as pubs, restaurants and places of worship.

> *'You must not meet socially with friends and family indoors*
> *in any setting unless you live with them or have formed*
> *a support bubble with them. This includes private homes, and*
> *any other indoor venues such as pubs and restaurants'.*

Within Tier 2 'High' alert level areas, it is still possible to meet outdoors with different households, but only in groups of six or fewer.

In addition, U.K. Prime Minister, Boris Johnson is expected to sign off on Tier 3 measures for parts of Northern England, with pressure being put on local leaders to accept the tighter restrictions.

There had been much speculation in recent days that London would be placed into a higher–level lockdown, with a rising infection rate and the city's Mayor, Sadiq Khan, calling for Tier 2 restrictions.

16th | United Kingdom

Prime Minister Boris Johnson has warned the 'situation in Greater Manchester is grave' and has urged its mayor Andy Burnham to 'reconsider and engage constructively' with the government after negotiations on putting the city into tighter restrictions turned sour.

In a televised press conference, Mr Johnson said that he was prepared to intervene to 'protect Manchester's hospitals and save the lives of Manchester residents' if no agreement could be reached with local leaders.

Mr Johnson said he 'completely' understands the reluctance of local leaders to move to Tier 3 restrictions but said that the situation in Greater Manchester 'worsens with each passing day'.

The Mayor of Greater Manchester Andy Burnham and other leaders in the region have so far opposed the region being placed into tier 3 restrictions. A key sticking point in reaching an agreement has been over the financial support package that is offered with the implementation of new restrictions; however, some leaders have also expressed concerns in recent days that proposed restrictions may not be effective.

On Thursday, Mr Burnham was described by many social media users as the 'King of the North' after opposing the tier 3 measures.

At the start of his press conference on Friday, Mr Johnson thanked the Metro Mayor of the Liverpool City Region Steve Rotheram, the Mayor of London Sadiq Khan and local leaders in Lancashire for working with the government to implement new restrictions.

The Labour Party and a growing number of other politicians and scientists have been calling on the U.K. government to implement a circuit–breaker lockdown to get the virus back under control, as is happening in Northern Ireland and is being considered in Wales. The Prime Minister has said he is ruling nothing out, but that 'it doesn't make sense' to lock down areas with low infection rates.

17th | New Zealand

New Zealand's Prime Minister, Jacinda Ardern, has been returned to office in a resounding victory over her rivals, winning nearly 50% of the vote – her National Party opponent has conceded defeat.

> 'New Zealand has shown the Labour Party its greatest support in almost 50 years [...] We will not take your support for granted. And I can promise you we will be a party that governs for every New Zealander'.

Ardern has been leading a minority government, with her Labour Party coming second in New Zealand's last general election in 2017. She became prime minister, despite not winning the most seats, by forming a minority coalition government with the New Zealand First Party and a confidence and supply arrangement that carried her government to an effective majority. No such coalition will be required this time though.

Ardern has made many headlines throughout her time in office, with her government bringing progressive reforms to New Zealand, such as increasing the minimum wage and significant environmental commitments.

She has also been prominent on the international stage, in 2018 becoming the second national leader to give birth whilst in office – after Benazir Bhutto – before attending a United Nations summit in New York with her new–born.

The following year she gained international attention again, following a massacre of worshippers at two Mosques in the South Island city of Christchurch. She was visibly moved by the events and grieved alongside all of those affected, before bringing in decisive gun reform that would prevent a similar tragedy from ever occurring again.

Her success as New Zealand's prime minister was only heightened throughout 2020 when she was incredibly successful in dealing with the coronavirus pandemic. New Zealand had amongst the fewest numbers of cases throughout the world and was noted for their incredible success; last week, there were more coronavirus cases reported amongst White House staff in the United States than the whole population of New Zealand. The country was quick to lock down and close their borders, since re–opening much of the country internally, with music festivals and sports events drawing envy from Europe and America.

The election had been due to take place in September and had been postponed due to the pandemic, though almost one–quarter of New Zealanders cast their ballot throughout the first two weeks of October when early voting opened.

New Zealand has a Parliamentary system, but instead of First Past the Post uses a Mixed Member Representation, where some list candidates are added to Parliament to reflect the popular vote, as well as there being MPs representing specific seats. The system was introduced in 1996 and no party has ever managed to secure the 61 seats required for a majority in the 24 years since.

Ardern however, looks set to achieve 64 seats in Parliament, making it a historic victory for her and her party.

With a renewed mandate and her popularity in no doubt her second term is likely to bring increasingly progressive reforms to the country, but blighted by economic crisis brought on by the coronavirus pandemic, the first majority in a quarter of a century could still provide the Prime Minister with significant challenges.

20th | Republic of Ireland

The Republic of Ireland has become the latest nation to announce that they are going into a new lockdown, with a second wave of coronavirus gripping much of Europe.

This comes just days after Northern Ireland and Wales announced that they were going to begin a 'circuit breaker' lockdown during the school half term, and a week after France implemented a curfew across many of its major cities.

Spain, the Netherlands, Denmark and Belgium have all gone into partial lockdown in recent weeks, whilst Germany has imposed new travel restrictions.

Most of Europe – with the exception of Sweden – now have significant measures in place, such as mandatory masks in indoor places and limits on gatherings – usually between 6 and 10 people.

Ireland's new lockdown goes further than most other European nations, with all non–essential shops closing and a 5km (3 mile) travel limit for exercise being imposed, aiming to limit the current trajectory of infection rates.

Much like in England, Ireland is using a tiered lockdown system; the country is set to move into its highest level for six weeks, which will prevent all social gatherings within households or gardens, except for tightly controlled weddings and funerals.

Taoiseach, Michaél Martin, announced the latest measures in an address to the nation;

> *'If we pull hard together over the next six weeks, we will have the opportunity to celebrate Christmas in a meaningful way.'*

Many of the highest infection rate areas within Ireland are around the border with Northern Ireland. The whole island of Ireland, and also Wales are now set to head into much tighter measures, and there is growing pressure on Westminster and Holyrood to act decisively to bring in tighter measures to disrupt the spread of the virus in England and Scotland.

Opposition leaders have been calling for a short, two–week circuit breaker, similar to those being imposed in Northern Ireland and Wales, with reports suggesting the SAGE committee had recommended such measures to Prime Minister Boris Johnson, who has instead placed certain high infection rate areas into Tier Two and Tier Three restrictions.

Ireland's current infection rate is 261 per 100,000 people, lower than those in England, Scotland, France and Spain; the government are also set to renew the wage subsidy for those who are unable to work due to the closures. People with average earnings over €400 a week and above will receive €350 (£320) a week, whilst subsidies are being put in place for businesses who are struggling to pay worker's wages.

23rd | Poland

Following a ruling by Poland's Constitutional Tribunal – one of the country's top courts – women no longer have the 'right to choose' in Poland. The termination of pregnancies will now only be permitted in cases where the mother's life is in danger, or in cases of rape and incest – around 2% of all cases.

As a heavily Catholic country – a religion that explicitly opposes abortion – Poland already had amongst the strictest abortion laws in Europe.

It is estimated that about 100,000 Polish women travel abroad each year in order to get around the tight restrictions, of what most European nations consider as a right.

Following the ruling, protests have erupted in major cities across the country, including Krakow, Lodz and Warsaw, the country's capital. It has been reported that police have been using tear gas and heavy force against what are believed to be peaceful protesters.

Hundreds of people marched from the Constitutional Tribunal Court to the home of Jaroslaw Kaczynski – who heads the governing Law and Justice party – to protest outside his house.

The Law and Justice Party (PiS) are a right–wing and socially conservative party – whose social views are far more extreme than most socially conservative parties in Europe. They won a second term in office in October 2019, and have been shifting the country towards greater social conservatism since their renewed mandate.

Whilst the court decision was made independently, PiS's stance is that taken by the court, with the party long opposing abortion. The case made its way to the Constitutional Tribunal following a legal challenge brought by the party against a 1993 law allowing abortion in cases of severe foetal disabilities.

The majority of the judges on the court were also appointed by PiS, with questions being raised as to the Court's neutrality and independence from Poland's government.

According to Antonina Lewandowska, a Polish sexual and reproductive health and rights activist, who spoke to the BBC, the defence of the 1993 law was based on UN rules outlawing torture. Protesters who gathered after the ruling carried signs bearing the words 'torture'; it is possible that the ruling could breach the European Convention on Human Rights (ECHR), or European Union law.

26th | United States

Joe Biden's campaign team have been clear in pushing the message 'vote and vote early'; under a backdrop of clear attempts by President Trump to try and undermine the legitimacy of postal voting and removing polling stations to make it harder for voters in mostly Democratic areas to cast their ballot.

Joe Biden's message is working, with young voters in particular, casting early votes in far greater numbers than in 2016, particularly in the vital swing states of Florida and the mid–western 'rust belt' states.

These record numbers have also seen videos all over social media showing lines snaking for block after block, with socially distanced voters itching to make their voice heard.

Yet, attempts of voter suppression are clear. Mostly black voters, in mid–western cities and typically in states that are going to be crucial on 3rd November, in lines stretching for hundreds of meters might be indicative of an enthusiasm to 'dump Trump', but is symptomatic of the systematic attempt by the Trump campaign to disenfranchise minority, mostly African American, voters.

Back in June, Donald Trump appointed Louis DeJoy – a significant Republican donor – to be postmaster general (head of the U.S. Postal Service) with the Trump supporter setting about to strip the United States Postal Service (USPS) of its resources and remove ballot–drops in many Democratic–leaning districts in swing states.

This has made postal voting harder for many, in a coronavirus afflicted election that was expected to make postal voting the norm, and instead, the Biden campaign has been encouraging people to cast their ballots in person, but to cast them early.

The lack of USPS resources and ballot–drops are not the only reason behind the huge lines at early voting polling stations, but the removal of polling stations; particularly in Texas.

Reports from many cities across the southern state have suggested that polling places are being taken away in cities with high minority populations (who are more likely to vote Democrat) making it harder for many people to cast a ballot. According to reports, more than 1200 polling places have been taken away across mostly southern states; most of these in areas with higher minority and particularly African American populations.

This also comes after polling last week suggested that some voters were being impacted by Trump's attempts to undermine the legitimacy of postal and proxy voting, through his frequent assertions that it might cause fraud (despite voting by post himself in the Republican primaries). Trump has frequently used White House press briefings to claim that postal voting is fraudulent, with suggestions that he is attempting to undermine the legitimacy due to the greater likelihood that Democratic voters will vote this way in November.

26th | United Kingdom

Outrage broke out after a Tesco store in Wales prohibited the sale of women's sanitary products after interpreting the Welsh government's guidelines to mean that they were non–essential.

The supermarket has blocked off aisles in their stores that sell toiletry products, such as toothpaste, shower gel and sanitary products, however, are still selling alcohol.

One Twitter user called out the supermarket for closing off these aisles, despite still selling alcohol, with the Tesco hierarchy who made the decision clearly not understanding the importance of sanitary products. Some have questioned the gender makeup of those involved in the decision if Tesco deemed sanitary products to be non–essential.

Supermarkets in Wales can still sell items that can be sold in pharmacies. Clothes, including babies' clothes, have also been deemed non–essential by the supermarket, whilst recent days have seen pictures of plastic wrapping covering products in the home section of Tesco and other supermarkets in an attempt to stop Welsh people from buying items not deemed as essential by the Welsh government.

26th | The Moon

There is water on the moon! According to NASA scientists, they have discovered water on the moon's sunlit surface, as well as pockets of ice in some of the shadow covered parts of the rock.

Although some evidence of water particles has been known since 2009, scientists now believe that there is a far greater prevalence than previously thought.

Speaking at a press conference, NASA scientists also spoke of an ambitious programme to land astronauts on the south pole of the lunar rock in 2024; this would be the first lunar visit since 1972.

27th | United States

In a controversial vote, Amy Coney Barrett has been confirmed to replace the late Justice Ruth Bader Ginsburg on the Supreme Court in a partisan 52–48 vote.

Barrett's confirmation, which was voted on last night, comes just 8 days before election day, with the Biden camp calling for the vote to be postponed until after the election due to the fact that 'more than 60 million Americans have already voted'.

The vote was controversial because Amy Coney Barrett was rushed through, only being selected as the nominee by President Trump last month (26th September).

In 2016, Justice Antonin Scalia passed away 8 months before the election, with Barack Obama nominating Merrick Garland to succeed him. Senate Republican leader Mitch McConnell refused to hold a confirmation hearing until after the election, and upon Donald Trump taking office, held a vote to appoint Trump nominee Neil Gorsuch to the Supreme Court instead.

Democrats had been calling on Republicans to delay the hearing due to the new precedent they had set in 2016, but despite the passing of Justice Ginsburg being just two months from election day, the Republican–controlled Senate rushed through Barrett to America's top bench.

Before passing, Justice Ruth Bader Ginsburg had called for her replacement to not be selected until after Americans had their say at the ballot box;

'[My] most fervent wish is that I will not be replaced until a new President is installed'.

Barrett is not just a controversial pick for the Supreme Court due to the perceived unfairness of her nomination, but for many of her conservative views, such as an opposition to women's 'right to choose', which although she has never ruled on, she has expressed her views on.

Her appointment gives the Supreme Court a 6–3 conservative lean, with 3 of the current justices being nominated by President Trump, an unprecedented number in a four-year term. In eight years, Obama had appointed just two: Sonya Sotomayor and Elena Kagan.

29th | United Kingdom

Former leader of the Labour Party, Jeremy Corbyn, has been suspended by the party over comments he made following the release of a report into the party by the Equalities and Human Rights Commission (EHRC).

An EHRC report was released to the public, with it containing damning indictments into the party's failure to deal with antisemitism during the leadership of Jeremy Corbyn. It was found that the party had broken the law in its handling of antisemitism under Corbyn's leadership.

It was announced that he had been suspended from the party some hours later, with many MPs in his own party welcoming the decision.

The EHRC report found that the party had been responsible for unlawful acts of harassment and discrimination. Many Jewish people left the party during Corbyn's tenure, including former MP, Luciana Berger. In a blog post following the release of the report, she wrote;

> *'I am grateful to the EHRC for its comprehensive investigation, which today finds the Labour Party guilty of harassment and committing unlawful acts relating to its Jewish members'.*

Jeremy Corbyn had rejected some of the findings in the report, with many of his supporters also rallying around the former party leader, with the hashtag #IStandWithJeremyCorbyn trending on Twitter throughout the morning.

Current Labour Leader, Keir Starmer, reacted to this by suspending his predecessor from the party, stating that;

> *'If – after all the pain, all the grief, and all the evidence in this report – there are still those who think there's no problem with antisemitism in the Labour party, that it's all exaggerated,*

Keir Starmer also stated that he was 'truly sorry' for the pain caused to the Jewish community. Corbyn has subsequently had the whip removed and will be sitting as an independent MP pending investigation.

The Equalities and Human Rights Commission investigation found evidence of antisemitic harassment and discrimination and said the party failed to take effective measures to stop 'antisemitic conduct'.

It found the Labour Party breached the Equality Act 2010, with party representatives using 'antisemitic tropes' and that many members (including at the leadership level) had suggested that complaints of antisemitism were fake or smears against the leadership.

29th | France

Three people have been killed in a knife attack in Nice, southern France, in what President Emmanuel Macron is calling an 'Islamist Terror Attack'.

A male suspect has been shot and detained following the attack. France has since raised their terror alert level and have deployed 4,000 troops to protect churches and schools in the country.

31st | United Kingdom

Boris Johnson has confirmed that England will enter a month–long period of new national lockdown.

Under the new measures, people will be required to stay at home, except for a limited number of reasons. People across the country will be banned from meeting others in indoor settings, and they can only meet one person from outside their household outdoors.

Educational settings will remain open during the lockdown, unlike in the Spring lockdown earlier this year, however, pubs, bars, restaurants, gyms, other entertainment and leisure venues and non–essential retail will all close. Takeaway and delivery outlets will be allowed to stay open.

The lockdown period will take place from Thursday the 5th of November and will end on Wednesday the 2nd of December 2020. Mr Johnson confirmed the new measures in a news conference from

Downing Street, after many details of a potential lockdown had already been leaked to the press.

The lockdown comes as COVID–19 is spreading rapidly throughout the country. The total number of cases recorded in the U.K. since the start of the pandemic has now surpassed one million, standing at 1,011,660.

The new measures are only for people in England – Northern Ireland, Scotland and Wales have different restrictions in place.

NOVEMBER

Lockdown Returns | Vaccine Hope

1st | United Kingdom

The government has said it is to extend the furlough scheme throughout the duration of November after it was announced that the U.K. is heading back into a national lockdown.

The scheme had been in place since March and has helped thousands of workers across the United Kingdom who have been unable to work due to the pandemic. Originally, the government had announced that the furlough scheme would end on the 31st of October, despite calls from across Parliament for the scheme to be extended, but the new national lockdown has meant that the government were somewhat forced to change course.

According to reports, many MPs within the Conservatives were unaware of the government's plan to extend furlough. Members of Johnson's Cabinet were also reportedly kept in the dark, despite the prime minister holding a Cabinet meeting via Zoom just hours before the announcement.

The mortgage repayment holidays have also been extended, with people entitled to up to six months' worth of holiday on their repayments without it affecting their credit score.

2nd | Austria

Just days after a terror attack in Nice, France, a similar attack has taken place in Vienna, Austria.

Four people were killed and a further 23 injured by a gunman, who had been described as having ISIL sympathies; the attack occurred in the 'Bermuda Triangle' area of the city, known for its nightlife.

Austria is currently under a midnight curfew due to the pandemic, and many were enjoying dinner and drinks before the attack at around 8pm local time.

The suspect was shot dead by police.

3rd | United States

The United States presidential election 2020 has crept up on us.

Despite being considered the most consequential election in decades by most Americans – not least by the Biden campaign – the pandemic election has become almost an afterthought to the virus itself. Yet, despite seeming a far more low–key affair than in a normal year, Americans are more fired up than ever and are likely to smash all turnout records.

Much of Joe Biden's campaign has focused on finding voters who did not vote last time but had voted for Obama in 2012. Hillary Clinton struggled, not because people voted for Trump in droves, but because her base did not turn up on the day, handing narrow victories to Trump in a number of key swing states.

Biden's campaign has focused on identifying these voters and getting them to 'vote, and vote early'. This has seen all early voting turnout records smashed, particularly amongst young people, who are the most likely demographic to vote Democratic. Key swing states Michigan, Pennsylvania, Wisconsin and Florida have seen as much as a 6–fold increase on early voting from 2016 amongst 18–29–year–old voters, showing that Biden is galvanising his base far more effectively than Clinton had done four years ago.

Florida has seen early and postal voting figures almost match the entirety of those who cast a ballot in 2016. With the coronavirus pandemic leading to many fearful of polling place queues (which in the United States can often be more than two hours long), there has been a rapid increase in those requesting postal ballots, or heading to the voting booth in the weeks before election day.

As they say, everything is bigger in Texas; this goes for voting too. Where Florida has almost matched its 2016 total before election day, Texas surpassed the total vote toll from 2016 days ago, with 10 million people casting ballots in the state, leading many to believe that it could actually swing Democratic for the first time since Jimmy Carter carried the state in 1976.

Polling still suggests that Trump should carry Texas and that Biden will carry many of the traditional swing states, with a healthy polling lead in Wisconsin, Michigan and Pennsylvania – all states that Trump won in 2016.

National polling is of course not important in the Electoral College, but the main difference from 2016 is enthusiasm. Whilst early voting was always likely to be higher than in 2016 due to the pandemic, the current projections show that voters are far more motivated than in previous years. High turnout elections tend to favour Democrats.

Whilst we may see fewer voters showing up on the day than usual, because so many have voted early, we are still likely to see an extremely high turnout election.

3rd | United States

Some early results are starting to come in from Kentucky and Indiana – the states whose polls closed first – and they are looking positive for Joe Biden.

Wabash County, Indiana, which was amongst the first to declare, fell heavily for Trump, by 70–28. However, in 2016 the result was 72–22 suggesting that Biden has gained significant ground on his Republican rival and that Democratic voter enthusiasm is up.

Polling throughout the day has also suggested that the result might favour Biden, with swing–state voters seeming to favour the Democratic candidate. However, the first Florida results being reported (at around 20%) Donald Trump has a slight lead, of around 50–48. This is likely to be election day voting, which Trump is believed to have an advantage in, with many Biden voters casting their ballots by post or casting them early.

There have already been some results called, with Kentucky and Indiana both being called for Trump, which would give him 18 Electoral College votes. These were always going to go to Trump, however, there have also been suggestions that Biden is making up significant ground in these states.

Vermont has been called for Biden; there are just three Electoral College votes there and it was always going to vote Democratic, with the party winning it in every election since 1988.

Some have been suggesting that the early results are even more favourable for Biden than the polls suggested and that the election could be a landslide, leading to it being called as early as 10 pm Eastern Standard Time, or by 3 am in the U.K.

However, with so few precincts reporting, results night is far from over and there are likely to be many more twists and turns before a clear winner emerges.

4th | United States

Despite Donald Trump announcing his intention to withdraw the United States from the Paris Climate Accords during the first year of his presidency, the United States has, today, officially left the agreement.

The exit from the agreement was one of the first major acts of Trump's presidency, where he seemingly sought to undo everything that President Obama had done during his eight years in office; efforts that saw him – unsuccessfully – attempt to overturn the Affordable Care Act, as well as a host of executive actions.

Should Trump lose the Presidential Election to Joe Biden, it is expected that the United States will immediately re–join the accords, with climate change action being one of the major planks of Joe Biden's agenda.

5th | United Kingdom

The United Kingdom has entered a second national lockdown after England joined with other parts of the United Kingdom to enter a full lockdown.

The measures are less strict than many in the previous lockdowns in the spring, but it is expected that they will still have a significant economic impact, with hospitality venues only available for takeaway.

Foreign Secretary Dominic Raab has today announced that he will go into self–isolation after a person he had been in contact with tested positive for the virus. This comes shortly after the news that China have placed a travel ban on those coming from the United Kingdom due to fears of increased cases in the country.

5th | United States

Joe Biden – more than two days after polls closed – looks set to win the 2020 election, despite the litigator–in–chief, Donald Trump, filing lawsuits to stop the counting of what all neutral and creditable arbiters consider legitimate votes. Yet with such a close election, the postmortem of why the Biden landslide did not come to fruition has already begun.

Predictions before Tuesday's election suggested that Biden would secure a strong – perhaps even historic – Electoral College victory, with all the swing states polling heavily in his favour and some red states even potentially being winnable for the former vice President. Yet, as things stand, he is sitting on 264 Electoral College votes, with

Nevada (worth six Electoral College votes) being too close to call, but expected to fall for Biden.

Joe Biden, although not securing a huge Electoral College victory, managed to secure the highest number of votes by any Presidential candidate in American history. In 2008, Barack Obama made history by achieving 69.4 million votes; surpassing the 62 million achieved by George W. Bush in 2004, but with some votes still yet to be counted, Joe Biden has smashed through the 70 million mark and in terms of raw numbers, massively surpassed the vote total of Hillary Clinton in the key swing states.

In Florida, Joe Biden has secured 5.3 million votes, almost 800,000 more than Clinton had achieved and had Trump not also had a massive increase in raw votes, he would have walked the state. If Trump secured the same number of votes in 2016, Biden would have won by almost half a million. What happened was not a Biden failure, but Trump causing another massive shock.

The same story is repeated in the mid–West; Biden has achieved more than 3 million in Pennsylvania, surpassing what Clinton achieved by around 200,000, enough to have won in 2016 and, with around 92% reporting, could still be enough for him to take the state this time.

He achieved more than 300,000 more votes in North Carolina than would have secured him a victory in 2016 and 400,000 more than Clinton had – yet in 2020 Trump looks set to win the state again. Even accounting for increases in population and demographic changes, Biden's campaign was extremely effective and in a 'normal' election year, would have walked into the White House with a striking majority.

The issue for Biden in the swing states that he lost does not seem to be because he could get the vote out and flip voters, but that Trump managed to secure huge increases on his 2016 result, perhaps due to a sophisticated voter targeting and data–based campaign.

Another fear is that the Republican Party was able to disenfranchise African American voters. In 2018, Stacey Abrams fought a tough race in the Georgia gubernatorial election, but there were cries of foul play after the Georgia Secretary of State (and her election opponent), Brian Kemp, had been purging legitimate voters from the voter rolls. Whilst purging voters is normal if, for example, voters have died or moved out of the state, there were irregularities.

The Georgia Secretary of State oversees the election for Governor and, in his role, Kemp had effectively overseen the legitimacy of his own election, which also saw him moving polling places with short notice (predominantly in African American neighbourhoods) and rejecting ballots that most other states would have considered legitimate. Although many of these concerns since 2018 have been addressed – Kemp introduced legislation regarding these once he had beaten Abrams in a tight race – there is a belief that many eligible voters were denied a vote and that many African Americans, particularly around Atlanta, had been disenfranchised.

The other major factor here though is that Donald Trump pulled off a shock. In 2016, he achieved 62.9 million votes, that's more than George Bush had achieved as the winner in 2004. Whilst he achieved a significant number of votes in 2016, he has grown that by almost 6 million.

Trump sits on 68.5 million votes currently, which would not just be the most ever achieved by a defeated Presidential candidate, but more than Hillary Clinton had achieved in the popular vote in 2016. Clearly, the Trump campaign were able to find new voters that they couldn't in 2016, even if Biden has managed to find even more.

This could be down to a number of reasons, the most likely being a sophisticated campaign. Whilst the headlines are taken by his rallies and the ridiculous dancing – set to the classic gay ballad, 'YMCA' – on his Twitter feed, his online campaign is perhaps the most sophisticated in history.

Biden may not have the landslide that many predicted, but he has also not failed as badly as has been suggested. He will still get across the line and has made history as the first to break the 70 million barrier; had the landscape not have changed so drastically in the last four years – and had there not been clear attempts to disenfranchise African American voters – he would have secured an historic Electoral College victory.

6th | United States

Donald Trump's presidency is coming to an end. The President spoke from the White House Press room this evening to rail against 'fake polls', which he called 'suppression polls' and claimed that the votes going against him are 'illegal'.

Speaking in a defeated and monotonous tone, a tired Trump took to the White House lectern repeatedly claiming (without evidence) that ballots being counted were 'illegal' and that he is preparing to bring more litigation, despite a number of lawsuits that his campaign brought being rejected by the courts.

This is against a backdrop of Georgia and Pennsylvania counting all outstanding ballots, with the results going heavily against Trump; it will be close, but it is likely that Biden will take Pennsylvania and possibly Georgia, taking him beyond the 270 needed to win.

Trump repeated many of the phrases that his personal attorney, Rudy Giuliani, had ranted about during a bizarre press conference yesterday, in which he stated that he would bring evidence of unfair and illegal practice in counting. This evidence is yet to be provided.

In his speech, Trump continually called for it to be a 'fair' result, suggesting that in his eyes, the only result that could be fair is one in which he wins, repeating a line used by his campaign staff throughout the election: 'in a free and fair election, Trump will win'.

By taking to the lectern, Donald Trump has perhaps indicated that the numbers his campaign team have access to suggest he is going to be defeated. The speech was a desperate attempt to undermine the legitimacy of the election in the face of defeat.

Many Republicans outside of the White House have been distancing themselves from Trump in recent days, with former ambassador to the UN under President Trump, Nikki Haley, stating that the integrity of the election was more important than Trump.

Senator Lindsay Graham and Senate Majority Leader, Mitch McConnell, have also refused to back the President, with the world lining up against Trump and showing that they believe the integrity of American democracy is far more important than one man.

The Trump administration is falling apart in real–time; American democracy is prevailing.

7th | United States

Four Seasons Total Landscaping – a small business in Northeast Philadelphia – was the sort of local, family–run business that few outside the Holmesburg neighbourhood would have known about. Yet on Saturday the 7th of November it became the sight of one of the weirdest and memorable press conferences of the Trump era.

The location, apparently deliberate and not just a mix up between a carpark and 4–star Four Seasons Hotel in the heart of Philadelphia, making it even more bizarre. The press conference was an unusual metaphor for the collapse of Trump's presidency, with his personal attorney, Rudy Giuliani, launching into a tirade about voter fraud over the ongoing count in key states – despite the fact that the only votes being counted were legitimately cast ones.

In the near forty–minute event, Giuliani made a number of unfounded allegations that reportedly had first emerged on pro–Trump blogs on the internet.

The press conference was widely panned, and contrasted significantly to the event held by now President–elect Biden, where he addressed a crowd of socially distanced cars and waiting global media. His victory speech, followed by a light show and fireworks, projected the hope and optimism that he had hoped his campaign – and election – would represent, marking a new and historic moment for America.

7th | United States

Joe Biden – a fresh–faced Senator with outdated ideas – announced his candidacy in the 1988 Presidential race from his home in Wilmington, Delaware. He was the youngest candidate amongst the Democratic field at just 44 years of age, but was heavily criticised for being too right–wing for the Democrats, spending much of his time in the Senate across the aisle with Republican colleagues. Now, in 2020 – 32 years later – he is preparing to take to the stage in the same city he first announced his Presidential ambitions, to speak as the oldest President–elect in American history.

Turning 78–years–old in just two weeks' time, Biden's presidency is significant for America on many levels, not just because of his age, but for the many records and firsts that his election to America's highest office represents.

Amongst the most notable is that in becoming President, his running mate, Kamala Harris, is the first woman and only the second person of colour to serve in national office in the U.S. Biden announced back in the final primary debate that he intended to play his part in breaking the glass ceiling by choosing a woman as his running mate and the important work of Hillary Clinton in her 2016 bid to become President has ensured that just four years later, this has been achieved. Biden's presidency may play an important role in paving the way for America to – at least in part – solve its problem of gender equality in the Oval Office.

When Harris was born, women had only been able to vote for 44 years, and many African Americans were still unable to vote. The Voting Rights Act 1965, the year after her birth, was a major step towards achieving racial equality and her election to America's second–highest office is another. 100 years after white women won the right to vote, America has finally elected a woman into the White House. Just 55 years after all African Americans were guaranteed the legal right to vote, the first person of colour has been elected to serve as vice President, and the first person of Indian descent has been elected to one of America's top offices.

The election of Kamala Harris is arguably the most historic moment of the 2020 election, but Joe Biden's election is historic in its own right. Although not as significant, he becomes the oldest person to ever become the President of the United States and only the second Catholic to be elected.

9th | Worldwide

Global cases of coronavirus have now surpassed 50 million. An estimate by Johns Hopkins University had said that the world had also reached 1.25 million deaths.

This is a significant increase in recent weeks, with a second wave of the virus responsible for at least a quarter of the cases and deaths. Around one–fifth of the deaths reported have been in Europe, with around 300,000 deaths on the continent.

In each of the last three days, the United States has reported more than 125,000 new cases, with the total now surpassing 10 million, and the number of deaths at around 200,000 – the highest total of a country in the world.

9th | Germany

Pharmaceutical company Pfizer have reached a major milestone in producing a vaccine that, according to preliminary trials, is 90% effective against COVID–19.

The company described it as a 'great day for science and humanity'. Pfizer, who were working with another company, BioNTech, plan on filing for emergency approval by the end of November, leading to some hope that there could finally be light at the end of the coronavirus tunnel.

The vaccine has been tested on 43,500 people across six countries and no safety concerns have been raised at this stage. Whilst there are around 10 vaccines currently in the final stages of development, this is the first one that has been proven to show positive results.

The stage of the trial, known as phase three, is vital in ensuring that the vaccine would be safe for the public, with the breakthrough following reports that there was a small chance of there being a vaccine by the end of the year.

The vaccine works by taking part of the COVID–19 virus' gene code and injecting it into the body, allowing the body to produce antibodies and develop immunity to the disease.

According to reports on the previous trials, this vaccine trains the body to produce the antibodies and the T–cells that the body needs in order to fight against a coronavirus infection.

Pfizer are hopeful that they can start to supply the vaccine this year, with upwards of 50 million doses available by the end of the year and potentially upwards of 1 billion throughout 2021. The major concern at this stage is that after beating the virus, the body tends to lose the antibodies needed to fight it very quickly, meaning that immunity may not last long. There are concerns over how long coronavirus immunity would last following receipt of the vaccine.

11th | United Kingdom

New guidance has been set out today to help manage university students travelling home for the Christmas period.

Students will be asked to follow the current nationwide lockdown restrictions in England until the 2nd of December, however, a 'student travel window' will run from the 3rd of December to the 9th, in which students will be allowed to travel home on staggered departure dates set by their university.

Through the student travel window, students will travel home following the four–weeks of national restrictions, which is hoped will reduce the risk of virus transmission to family and friends in their home cities.

The government has also said that coronavirus tests will be offered to as many students as possible before they travel home for Christmas, with universities in areas of a particularly high prevalence of the virus being prioritised. Students who test positive ahead of their departure will need to remain in self–isolation for ten days.

As a result, all university teaching will need to be moved online by 9 December, and potentially earlier, to allow for students travelling home.

11th | Hong Kong

A number of pro–democracy lawmakers in Hong Kong have resigned after a new law was passed by the Chinese government in Beijing effectively banning opposition; four of their colleagues from the Hong Kong legislative council were removed just hours later.

The Hong Kong legislature – which was already stacked heavily in favour of pro–Beijing lawmakers – had four pro–democracy legislators removed as the semi–autonomous region continues to be brought closer under the control of Beijing.

Beijing imposed a law on Wednesday that allowed for the removal of any legislators that they branded as 'unpatriotic', with four legislators from the pro–democracy faction being removed with immediate effect. The remainder of the pro–democracy lawmakers then resigned after the move, meaning that there is almost no opposition to Beijing left within the Hong Kong legislature.

This comes just months after Beijing imposed a new security law upon Hong Kong, which allowed the Chinese Communist Party (CCP) to criminalise any activity they believed to be 'secession, subversion and collusion with foreign forces'.

The Security Law – passed in June 2020 – was an attempt to prevent the protests that had gripped Hong Kong in recent years over the continued decline of democracy in the country and the erosion of the distinct political and legal system that Hong Kong was supposed to have from China following the handover from British rule.

Hong Kong was formerly a British colony, returned to Chinese rule in 1997, but retaining some autonomy from Beijing under 'one country, two systems' until 2047. This move means that the legislature now almost entirely resides in the hands of pro–CCP lawmakers, who are able to exercise almost complete control over the territory.

The chairman of the Hong Kong Democratic Party, Wu Chi–wai, stated: 'We can no longer tell the world that we still have 'one country, two systems', this declares its official death'.

Amongst those removed from the legislature were the Civic party's Alvin YE.U.ng, Kwok Ka–ki and Dennis Kwok and Kenneth LE.U.ng of the Professionals Guild. All of these lawmakers had already been barred from running in legislative elections originally scheduled for September.

U.K. Foreign Secretary Dominic Raab said;

> *'This campaign to harass, stifle and disqualify democratic opposition tarnishes China's international reputation and undermines Hong Kong's long–term stability'.*

The new law creates an effective ban on anyone who supports independence from sitting in the Hong Kong legislature. The law – passed by Beijing's highest legislative body – also means that anyone who refuses to recognise Beijing's sovereignty over Hong Kong or seeks help from 'foreign countries or foreign forces to interfere in the affairs of the region' will be removed from office.

As with the Security Law, passed in June, there is a fear that the ambiguity in this legislation means that the CCP can remove and (under the Security Law) potentially prosecute any political opponents within the Hong Kong legislature, meaning that the system of two separate systems is effectively ended.

The remaining 15 pro–democracy legislators appeared before the press following the removal of their colleagues, holding hands and chanting, before announcing that they would resign on Thursday.

13th | United Kingdom

Chief Adviser to the prime minister, Dominic Cummings has left his role at Number 10 Downing Street with immediate effect.

Mr Cummings was seen leaving Downing Street holding a storage box just hours after a government minister indicated Mr Cummings would leave his role by the end of the year.

It had been believed that Mr Cummings, and Director of Communications Lee Cain who also resigned this week, would both stay on until Christmas – however, both have reportedly now vacated their roles immediately.

Earlier in the day, Mr Cummings claimed, 'rumours of me threatening to resign are invented'. Over recent days, a number of MPs have called for the departure of Mr Cummings, including senior Conservative backbencher Sir Roger Gale. On Thursday, Mr Gale tweeted, 'The time has come in the interest of the country that Mr Cummings is seen out through the door immediately'.

Mr Cummings has long been a controversial figure and also one seen to be particularly influential at Downing Street. His departure, along with the resignation of Lee Cain, could spark significant change within the team around Boris Johnson at Downing Street, at a key time with the coronavirus pandemic ongoing and the end of the Brexit transition period taking place next month.

17th | United Kingdom

Former leader of the Labour Party, Jeremy Corbyn, has been reinstated to the party following the decision last month to suspend him, however, the party leader, Keir Starmer, will not reinstate the whip – meaning he will have to sit in Parliament as an independent MP.

The Islington MP had been suspended since October for his response to an Equality and Human Rights Commission (EHRC) investigation into Labour's handling of antisemitism complaints.

The decision to suspend Corbyn had been taken by the parties' general secretary, David Evans, but was seen to be supported by current Labour leader, Keir Starmer, who criticised Corbyn for his response to the EHRC report.

Starmer's said that his decision not to reinstate the whip was due to Corbyn undermining trust in the party's ability to tackle anti–Semitism.

> 'Jeremy Corbyn's actions in response to the EHRC report undermined and set back our work in restoring trust and confidence in the Labour Party's ability to tackle antisemitism'.

His decision has been welcomed by many Jewish members of the Labour Party who were left angered by the NEC decision to reinstate Corbyn.

17th | Moldova

Maia Sandu, the former prime minister, has become Moldova's first female President, claiming an overwhelming victory with 57.7% of the vote.

She defeated incumbent Igor Dodon, who had spent much of the campaign attacking her with sexist remarks, primarily attacking her for not being married, or having had children.

Moldova has amongst the worst gender gaps – meaning a disparity in wealth and social equality between genders – in Europe, the 23rd highest in the world, and Sandu's election is seen as a significant step for the country.

Her election is also significant as she is considered far more pro–European than her predecessor, with Dodon being more aligned with Russia.

Russian President Vladimir Putin congratulated Sandu following her victory.

She had served as prime minister from June 2019 – November 2019, when she was ousted in a no–confidence vote. She had previously run for the presidency in 2016, but was defeated by Igor Dodon.

18th | United Kingdom

The U.K. government has received criticism in recent months over £17 billion being paid in contracts to a series of companies in relation to the coronavirus response.

Criticism has focused on the lack of oversight in awarding the contracts, with many suggesting that companies who donate to the Conservative Party – often with little or no experience in the contract they are performing – are being favoured.

Whilst there is currently little evidence that this is the case, the government have received criticism for the lack of transparency in their decision making, and a number of errors, that have led to unfulfilled orders and quality control catastrophes.

For example, Former Cabinet Office minister and current Conservative life peer saw a £1 million contract go to a firm that he was – until recently – a major shareholder of, with concerns about undue influence being wielded and allowing the government to offer contracts to those they have personal ties with.

Whilst there is not necessarily any wrong doing at this stage, it is clear that there is a concerning lack of transparency in the decision making; at the very least, it looks like bias; at the worst, it could be blatant cronyism.

19th | United States

Since Donald Trump's defeat in the U.S. Presidential Election, his personal attorney, Rudy Giuliani, has made bizarre press conferences a feature of the outgoing President's collapse. Yet perhaps none have been weirder than Rudy Giuliani's face appearing to melt whilst berating reporters.

In what has been a sad attempt to overturn democracy, the president's legal team – spearheaded by Giuliani – has launched a tirade of legal challenges to stop the country of perfectly legal votes that had gone against Trump.

He was giving an update on these legal efforts when, under the hot white lights of media cameras, beads of brown liquid began rolling down his cheeks. They weren't forced tears for a dying presidency, but streaks of hair dye running down his face.

At the press conference, Giuliani was trying to present evidence of what he considered to be voter fraud, despite admitting he currently had no evidence at this time. He said it was not about singular voter fraud in any one state, but some greater existential voter fraud that seemed to exist outside the realm of tangible evidence.

However, nobody could pay attention to Giuliani's bizarre efforts; they were too distracted by his face.

20th | United Kingdom

The U.K. government's independent adviser on standards Sir Alex Allan has resigned after Prime Minister Boris Johnson backed Home Secretary Priti Patel following a bullying inquiry.

The Prime Minister has ruled that Priti Patel did not breach the ministerial code, following an inquiry into bullying allegations against her. Sir Alex Allan, who authored the inquiry's report has since resigned.

In a statement, Sir Allan said;

> *'I feel that it is right that I should now resign from my position as the Prime Minister's independent adviser on the code'.*

It is understood that in the report, Sir Allan found Ms Patel's approach on occasions 'amounted to behaviour that can be described as bullying'.

An investigation into bullying allegations against Home Secretary Priti Patel was launched in March, less than a month after the resignation of the Home Office's most senior civil servant, Sir Philip Rutnam. Sir Rutnam's resignation came at a time of multiple allegations about Ms Patel's behaviour.

Ms Patel has released a statement saying she was sorry 'that my behaviour in the past has upset people'.

21st | United Kingdom

With the night's drawing in, there was light at the end of the tunnel; the prime minister had stated back in the summer that he hoped the country would be back closer to normality by Christmas. Yet as the United Kingdom was forced back into lockdown by rising infection rates and the highest death toll since the spring, the light at the end of the tunnel was snatched away. But whilst Britons were waking up to dark, frost carpeted mornings in their homes, the vaccine arms race was heating up.

The first out of the block were Pfizer, their vaccine – made in collaboration with BioNTech – was announced to be 90% effective in preliminary trials. The government hastily gathered a press conference for the video linked journalists, and the waiting public at home, to announce that they had pre–ordered 40 million doses and could start vaccinating by Christmas; there might now – finally – be an end in sight.

Just days later, from across the Atlantic, more good news came when Moderna announced that they had developed a vaccine too, this time 95% effective. The vaccine does not require the same –70– degree storage temperatures that the Pfizer–BioNTech vaccine did, leading to hope that it may be much easier to roll out en masse. In another hasty press conference, Health Secretary, Matt Hancock, stated that the government had already secured 5 million doses and were hoping for more in the coming months; to the delight of many Conservative backbenchers, the E.U. had secured none.

Then, even more good news came when the alma mater of the health secretary, the chancellor of the exchequer and the prime minister announced that they too had made a breakthrough. The horse that the government had backed from the beginning, Oxford University, announced;

> 'The ChAdOx1 nCov–2019 coronavirus vaccine [...] has been shown to trigger a robust immune response in healthy adults aged 56–69 and those over 70 years of age. The data, published today in The Lancet, suggest that one of the groups most vulnerable to serious illness, and death from COVID–19, could build immunity'.

The Oxford University vaccine is at an earlier stage than both Pfizer and Moderna and the university have announced that they believe it is unlikely they will start to take it to market until 2021, however, Pfizer – who have now applied for approval from the American Food and Drug Authority – are expecting to start vaccinating people within the next month, likely from mid–December. Moderna too, are likely to bring their product to market before the turn of the year, although the supply numbers are likely to be low.

The need for −70−degree storage temperatures means that it is likely going to be a logistical challenge to roll out the Pfizer vaccine on a large scale, and perhaps will only be used until a more efficient product is brought to market. Although the government have ordered 40 million doses, patients would require two shots of the vaccine to be protected and it is likely that delivery of this many would not be possible until late next year. As such, it may be used in the early stages and then a switch to a less logistically challenging vaccine could be seen.

With three potential options on the market in a matter of months, it is likely that by spring or summer 2021, most people will be able to get vaccinated, allowing for people to go somewhat back to normal life.

25th | United Kingdom

A foreign office minister has resigned following the announcement of a cut to the U.K.'s foreign aid budget.

Baroness Sugg, a junior minister who has served as the Minister for Overseas Territories and Sustainable Development since February this year, has resigned after the foreign aid budget was cut to 0.5% of Gross National Income (GNI).

In her resignation letter to the prime minister, Baroness Sugg said;

> 'I believe it is fundamentally wrong to abandon our commitment to spend 0.7% of gross national income on development. This promise should be kept in the tough times as well as the good'.

In their 2019 General Election manifesto, the Conservatives had committed to funding the foreign aid budget at the equivalent of 0.7% of gross national income.

Announcing the decision to cut the budget on Wednesday, Chancellor Rishi Sunak told MPs that sticking to the 0.7% would be 'difficult to justify' to the British public in light of the economic consequences of the coronavirus pandemic.

A number of MPs have criticised the decision, including Shadow Chancellor Anneliese Dodds. Former prime ministers David Cameron and Tony Blair also warned against the decision before it was announced.

In 2016, the U.K. spent £13.4 billion on overseas aid, in line with its commitment of 0.7% of gross national income. Foreign aid spending supports a range of projects helping the world's poorest populations. The money has previously been spent on humanitarian aid, crisis relief and bilateral aid through organisations such as the United Nations.

DECEMBER

2nd | United Kingdom

The Pfizer–BioNTech vaccine has been approved for emergency use by the Medicines and Healthcare Products Regulatory Authority (MHRA), meaning that it could be rolled out as early as next week.

This is the first vaccine against COVID–19 to be approved anywhere in the world following phase three trials and the United Kingdom will be the first country to start rolling out vaccines. Health Secretary Matt Hancock suggested that as many as 800,000 doses could be available by next week.

Pfizer said that the first doses will arrive in the coming days, with the U.K. having ordered 40 million doses, the majority of which will arrive throughout the first half of 2021. Patients will require two doses for the vaccine to be effective, meaning that the Pfizer–BioNTech vaccine could be used to vaccinate around a third of the U.K. population, based on the current quantity ordered

Matt Hancock said that the first doses would be given to the most vulnerable people. He added;

'This is a momentous occasion and provides fresh hope that we can beat this pandemic, with the UK at the forefront of this revolutionary breakthrough.'

This vaccine, however, does present significant challenges in being rolled out, needing to be stored at –70 degrees Celsius and posing significant logistical issues. Matt Hancock said that some hospitals and doctors' surgeries with the appropriate cold storage facilities may stock the vaccine, but mobile and pop–up centres may not be suitable.

2nd | United Kingdom

Fans will be allowed back into sports stadiums, after Boris Johnson gave the green light for a return after the November lockdown ended today.

The prime minister has permitted up to 4,000 fans, or 50% capacity (whichever is lowest), to return to stadiums in Tier 1 areas, although fans will still be prevented from attending games in Tier 3. In Tier 2, the capacity will be either 2,000 or 50%, whichever is lower.

It was also announced that indoor venues, such as gyms, theatres and concert halls will also be permitted to re–open, provided that there are capacity limits.

2nd | United Kingdom

What is a substantial meal? It is a question that we are all wondering now the government have said that drinking alcohol must be accompanied by a substantial meal when the country is released back into a tiered system today.

The government's guidelines on what constitutes substantial is being widely criticised as being too vague; does a sandwich equal a meal, what about a scotch egg?

Communities Secretary Robert Jenrick seemed to suggest that a substantial meal is one that would be the major meal of the day, meaning that there would be no 'packet of crisps' or 'side of fries' loopholes that would allow punters to drink as normal at their usual watering holes.

3rd | United Kingdom

Prime Minister Boris Johnson has announced a new target to reduce the U.K.'s emissions by at least 68% by 2030 compared to 1990 levels.

The new target is an NDC (Nationally Determined Contribution) under the Paris Climate Change Agreement. Under the agreement signed in 2015, countries are obliged to update their commitments to cut emissions and deliver an NDC by the end of 2020. The U.K. is the first major economy to have announced its new NDC and the announcement comes ahead of the U.K. co–hosting the Climate Ambition Summit next weekend, five years on from the Paris Agreement.

It is hoped that the new NDC will encourage other countries to set similar targets. NDCs are a key part of the Paris Agreement to hold global temperature increases well below 2 degrees.

Currently, the U.K. is targeting achieving net zero emissions by 2050.

'Today, we are taking the lead with an ambitious new target to reduce our emissions by 2030, faster than any major economy, with our Ten Point Plan helping us on our path to reach it'. – Boris Johnson

Business and Energy Secretary and COP26 President Alok Sharma said that the U.K.'s new emissions target is 'among the highest in the world and reflects the urgency and scale of the challenge our planet faces'.

4th | United Kingdom

Liverpool's mayor, Joe Anderson, has been arrested by police on Friday, it is understood.

In a statement released by Merseyside Police, it was said that five men have been arrested as part of an investigation into the awarding of building and development contracts in Liverpool.

3 men aged 62, 33 and 46 years old have been arrested on suspicion of conspiracy to commit bribery and witness intimidation, while two other men aged 25 and 72 years old have been arrested on suspicion of witness intimidation.

In the statement, Merseyside Police said the individuals were taken to police stations across Merseyside for questioning by detectives.

The identity of those arrested has not been officially announced, though the 62–year–old is reported to be Mr Anderson, the city's directly–elected mayor.

According to reports, Mr Anderson has been suspended from the Labour Party pending the outcome of the police investigation. Liverpool City Council has said it is co–operating with Merseyside Police.

Mr Anderson has been the mayor of Liverpool since 2012, before which he was the leader of Liverpool City Council since 2010 and a councillor since 1998.

7th | United Kingdom

Prime Minister and E.U. Commission President have said that conditions for finalising a post–Brexit U.K.–E.U. trade deal are 'not there'.

Prime Minister Boris Johnson and Commission President Ursula von der Leyen spoke after negotiators carried out a further effort to try and find a breakthrough over the weekend.

In a joint statement following the call, Boris Johnson and Ursula von der Leyen said;

> *'As agreed on Saturday, we took stock today of the ongoing negotiations. We agreed that the conditions for finalizing an agreement are not there due to the remaining significant differences on three critical issues: level playing field, governance and fisheries'.*

While the U.K. left the European Union on 31st January this year, it is currently in a transition period in which it remains part of some E.U. institutions including the single market and customs union.

The transition period is set to end on 31st December 2020 – if no deal is agreed and ratified by both sides by this point, the U.K. will have to trade with the E.U. on World Trade Organization terms.

8th | United Kingdom

The U.K. has begun the biggest vaccination programme in NHS history as the first patients receive the Pfizer/BioNTech COVID–19 vaccine.

Margaret Keenan, who is a grandmother and turns 91 next week, was the first person in the world to be given the vaccine, being given the injection at 06:31 this morning.

The momentous day of the vaccine starting to be rolled out, dubbed as V–Day by Health Secretary Matt Hancock, comes just 311 days after the first case of the virus was confirmed in the Prime Minister Boris Johnson has thanked NHS staff, scientists and all those involved in the development and distribution of the vaccine.

In a teary interview on Good Morning Britain, Matt Hancock said seeing the vaccine being rolled out made him 'so proud to be British'.

The second patient and first man to receive the vaccine was William Shakespeare, an 81–year–old from Warwickshire.

The U.K. is the first country to start using the Pfizer/BioNTech vaccine after approving it for use last week. Around 800,000 doses of the vaccine are expected to be dispensed in the coming weeks, while up to four million more are expected by the end of December.

First to receive the vaccine will be health and care staff and over 80–year–olds.

While it is hoped the rollout of the vaccine will allow a rapid return to something closer to normality in the coming months, people are being warned that the virus is still deadly and that they should continue following coronavirus restrictions.

9th | Belgium

U.K. Prime Minister Boris Johnson is to have dinner with E.U. Commission President Ursula von der Leyen in Brussels this evening to continue discussions regarding a post–Brexit U.K.–E.U. trade deal.

Ms von der Leyen has said 'I look forward to welcoming' Mr Johnson to Brussels, though the discussions on the menu this evening are expected to be much more than a standard diplomatic formality. The end of the Brexit transition period on 31 December is fast–approaching, with time really running out in the search for a post–Brexit trade agreement to be reached between the U.K. and E.U.

Post–Brexit trade negotiations have been taking place throughout the year, following the U.K.'s official departure from the European Union on January 31, 2020. However, negotiations have repeatedly got stuck on key differences including the level playing field, governance and fisheries.

The talks this evening are to see whether the leaders may still be willing to compromise on some points to get technical talks moving again. If the leaders cannot agree to consider more compromises and budging on some of their positions, talks will likely break down, leading towards a no–deal scenario.

9th | United States

Social media giant Facebook is facing two separate lawsuits in the United States which are accusing the company of abusing its power.

The U.S. Federal Trade Commission (FTC) and a coalition of more than 40 state prosecutors are suing the company, claiming that it has acted illegally to buy up rivals and stifle competition in the market.

In a series of tweets, New York Attorney General Letitia James said;

'We are taking action to stand up for the millions of consumers and many small businesses that have been harmed by Facebook's illegal behavior'.

The lawsuits being filed against Facebook mainly focus on their 2012 acquisition of Instagram and 2014 purchase of WhatsApp. Both of the acquisitions were previously looked at by the FTC and were approved, but officials are now asking the court to consider breaking up the company.

Facebook has said in a statement, 'We look forward to our day in court, when we're confident the evidence will show that Facebook, Instagram and WhatsApp belong together, competing on the merits with great products'.

The company has also claimed that the lawsuits could harm consumers and innovation. The lawsuits come after the U.S. Justice Department sued Google back in October, claiming that the company had abused its market power.

14th | India

Whilst the United Kingdom is wrapped in a news cycle on delivering a Brexit deal before Christmas – threatening French fishermen with gunboats – and Germany is sent back into lockdown, there has been little news coverage on the ongoing farmers strike in India, where there are an estimated quarter of a billion people protesting.

That is more than the population of Germany, France and the United Kingdom combined, all taking part in a demonstration against the Indian government, with roads and infrastructure into some major cities being blocked off, bringing much of the country to a halt.

The strike that is currently ongoing is the latest demonstration after weeks of protests across the country, with the Indian government – led by Prime Minister Narendra Modi – ending subsidies for Indian farmers. Instead, the government are planning on allowing private buyers greater power to set prices, potentially limiting the price that farmers will get for their products.

Almost half of India's workforce are in farming, with the subsidies ensuring that many can make–ends–meet, with margins often extremely small in the industry; the ending of subsidies could damage the livelihoods of many farmers.

For almost 60 years, the Indian government has guaranteed a minimum price for certain crops, ensuring that farmers are able to receive some remuneration for their products and not be exploited by low prices. It is believed that these subsidies played a significant role in the economic development of the country, lifting many families out of poverty since the 1960s.

The changes do not eradicate the guaranteed minimum prices; however, they do get remove restrictions on corporations buying land and stockpiling commodities beyond a certain level, which often makes it difficult for smaller farmers to compete. The coronavirus pandemic saw many smaller–scale operations struggle due to the infrastructure and supply chain issues that were presented, resulting in them falling behind larger farms; there is a fear the law changes will worsen this.

The new laws also prevent stubble burning – a practise where farmers burn a recently harvested field to make it quicker to plant a new crop – which has been criticised by many farmers.

Protests broke out some weeks ago, with demonstrations around some of the countries' major cities, with a march on Delhi beginning at the end of November and continuing into December. They were met by armed police once they arrived in Delhi, with many protesters being tear–gassed and water cannoned, prompting solidarity protests from Indian communities across much of Europe and North America.

A number of farmers groups have however supported the measures, making it perhaps unlikely that the farmers will manage to achieve significant concessions from the Modi government. Many regional government officials are also negotiating with the farmers, but protests are likely to continue for some time.

16th | United Kingdom

There is a 'unanimous agreement' between the U.K. government and devolved administrations that the U.K.–wide easing of restrictions over the Christmas period should still go–ahead, Boris Johnson has told MPs.

Ministers had been facing calls to rethink the planned easing of restrictions for a five–day period between 23–27 December, with cases of COVID–19 currently rising sharply in many parts of the U.K.

Labour Leader Sir Keir Starmer, London Mayor Sadiq Khan and other politicians had called for the Christmas coronavirus rules to be reviewed.

On the topic of the eased restrictions over Christmas, a rare joint editorial on Tuesday from the British Medical Journal and Health Service Journal said: 'We believe the government is about to blunder into another major error that will cost many lives'.

However, following talks between the governments of all four U.K. nations, people will still be able to form Christmas 'bubbles' with up to two other households and travel restrictions will still be lifted across the U.K. during the five–day period. The exact policies are now though differing across the four U.K. nations.

It is understood though that there will be increased messaging over the next week to warn people about the risks of coming into contact with other people. While Boris Johnson has said an agreement has been reached over the regulations across the U.K., the advice appears to differ slightly across the U.K. nations.

19th | United Kingdom

The prime minister has announced major new restrictions in England due to significant concerns over a new variant of COVID–19.

London and parts of the South East and East of England which are currently in Tier 3 will move into a new set of restrictions after unlocking a previously unseen level – Tier 4. This new tier will largely represent the measures in place during England's nationwide lockdown in November.

In Tier 4 areas, non–essential retail outlets, leisure facilities and personal care services must all close. People must stay at home except for a limited number of reasons set out in law and people should work from home wherever possible. The new measures will take effect from Sunday morning.

New guidance and restrictions on travel will also be introduced. People in Tier 4 areas should not leave Tier 4 areas and will not be permitted to travel abroad except for a limited number of reasons, such as for essential business.

People living in Tier 1, 2 & 3 areas are advised to avoid international travel and 'stay local'.

Major changes have also been announced to the plans for the easing of restrictions over Christmas. In Tier 4 areas, there will be no easing of restrictions and people will not be able to meet with others in indoor settings, except in their existing support bubble. People in these areas will only be allowed to meet with one person from outside their household in an outdoor public place.

In the rest of England, the easing of restrictions over the Christmas period, which had been planned for five days, will now just take place on one day – Christmas Day.

Announcing the new measures, Boris Johnson said 'We cannot continue with Christmas as planned'. He also emphasised the importance for people to follow the rules on New Year's Eve and New Year's Day.

Mr Johnson said that the new strain of COVID–19 could be up to 70% more transmissible, according to early data.

19th | United Kingdom

Scotland – along with Wales and England – have announced a tightening of lockdown restrictions throughout Christmas, marking a sharp U–turn from the planned 5–day travel period that would allow families to meet up.

Speaking at a press conference, First Minister Nicola Sturgeon announced that the 5–day window to meet up would now only be for Christmas day, meaning that families will not be able to stay over in separate households during Christmas.

Scotland is also introducing a travel ban, with a strict ban on anyone entering the country from the rest of the United Kingdom, hoping to prevent a further spread of a new strain of coronavirus – that spreads up to 70% more rapidly than the original virus – from entering the country.

The country will also bring forward a national 'Tier 4' lockdown for Scotland from Boxing Day, having originally planned to implement it on the 28th December, after the Christmas travel period ended. This is a far tighter level of restriction that is largely equivalent to a full lockdown, like those seen throughout the United Kingdom in the Autumn.

19th | United Kingdom

Prime Minister Boris Johnson, in the press conference to announce the cancellation of Christmas, also revealed details about a new strain of coronavirus, following an emergency Cabinet meeting.

There will be a swathe of new restrictions in place in the coming days as a result of the new strain, which will see London and the South East placed into tougher restrictions.

A new strain of the coronavirus was discovered in Kent in recent weeks, which is believed to be up to 70% more transmissible than the old variant and is becoming the dominant strain in parts of the country.

There is now an end to the Christmas travel window in these areas, with households now no longer able to mix, despite the prime minister assuring the country that these would remain in place just days ago.

It is expected that governments in other parts of the U.K. will take similar action in the coming days.

Scenes of people flooding train stations in an attempt to escape the new restrictions have emerged on social media, with people in London fleeing to get home to areas where there will not be such harsh restrictions, for the Christmas period.

There are fears that by making the changes so late, people will now be stranded in some locations, with many forced to spend Christmas Day alone and without loved ones. Many support the restrictions, but are critical of the government's timing, with it being alleged that the new variant was discovered in September and that the government were aware of it for many weeks.

The government first announced that the strain had been identified on 14th December, five days before the announcement on new restrictions.

20th | United Kingdom

Labour Leader Sir Keir Starmer has responded to the prime minister's announcement of new coronavirus restrictions in England by supporting the measures but criticising Mr Johnson for waiting 'until the eleventh hour' to make the decision.

Speaking at a Labour Party press conference, Sir Keir said, 'Sadly, the measures the government announced yesterday are necessary and we support them'. Starmer also urged people to follow the new restrictions but said he understood the upset, saying, 'I know the hurt people are feeling – and the anger – because Christmas is more than just a holiday. It is a part of who we are as a nation'.

Starmer criticised the prime minister for dismissing warnings and not acting sooner, saying 'the alarm bells have been ringing for weeks, but the Prime Minister chose to ignore them'.

21st | United Kingdom

Boris Johnson has said that he understands the concerns of the U.K.'s international friends and partners about the new strain of COVID–19 and that the U.K. government is working with others to unblock cross channel trade as soon as possible. This follows news that France have prevented channel crossing, leaving hundreds of lorries stranded in Kent.

Prime Minister Boris Johnson has said that delays are only occurring at Dover and only human–handled freight are being affected. According to Mr Johnson, this is only around 20% of U.K. freight arriving from or going to the European continent.

Mr Johnson said that he had 'a very good call' with French President Emmanuel Macron earlier on Monday afternoon and that teams are working hard to resolve the problems.

Around 170 lorries were stuck at Dover on early Monday evening, though around 500 were stuck at the peak of the disruption.

It comes after many countries have cancelled flights to and from the U.K., while France has temporarily shut its border with the U.K. over fears of the new strain of the virus.

22nd | Antarctica

Throughout the coronavirus pandemic, that had impacted almost the entire world, one place had remained untouched, Antarctica. That was until now.

An outbreak of COVID–19 has impacted 36 people stationed at a Chilean research base on the Antarctic continent.

All 36 people, which includes 26 members of the Chilean army and 10 maintenance workers, have since been evacuated to Chile, where they are self–isolating and reported to be in a good condition.

Research on the continent has been halted during the pandemic, in an attempt to keep the continent free of the virus.

Although the continent is not permanently inhabited, there will be as many as 100 residents at any given time, typically researchers carrying out varied work throughout the winter.

23rd | South Africa

Another new variant of COVID–19 has been identified, emerging from South Africa, with two cases so far confirmed in the U.K., Health Secretary Matt Hancock has said.

Both of the cases of the latest variant are being linked to travel to South Africa, where the variant is much more widespread. As a result, the U.K. has implemented travel restrictions with South Africa.

Anyone in the U.K. who has visited South Africa in the past 14 days, and anyone they have been in contact with, are being told to self–isolate immediately.

Like the Kent variant, it is believed to be far more transmissible than the original virus. The full significance of the new strain of the virus is not yet known, though the new strain is now thought to be the dominant form of COVID–19 in parts of South Africa, which has experienced rapid increases in cases recently.

The Foreign, Commonwealth and Development Office is currently advising against all but essential travel to the whole of South Africa.

24th | United Kingdom

Just days before the end of the transition period, the U.K. and the E.U. have struck a post–Brexit trade deal.

The achievement of a deal comes after months of missed deadlines and multiple points where talks looked likely to collapse.

The U.K. left the European on the January 31st of 2020, under the Withdrawal Agreement – the new trade treaty will take over from the arrangements that have been in place since then under the transition period where the U.K. has had to continue to follow many E.U. rules.

The treaty will apply from 1st of January 2021, though it still needs to be ratified by both sides.

It has been confirmed that MPs in the House of Commons will debate and vote on the post–Brexit trade deal on Wednesday the 30th of December. The Speaker of the House of Commons, Sir Lindsay Hoyle has granted a request from the government to recall the House from 09:30 on 30 December, just hours after the announcement of a post–Brexit trade deal being reached between the U.K. and the E.U.

The House of Lords will meet at midday on the same day. Parliament is currently in recess, but under Standing Orders, the Speaker of the Commons can decide to recall the House if ministers have made a case to him that doing so is in the public interest.

28th | United Kingdom

The post–Brexit trade agreement between the U.K. and E.U. has moved a step closer to being passed after it was unanimously approved by E.U. ambassadors.

Ambassadors for E.U. member states backed a provisional application of the agreement, according to a spokesperson for the German E.U. Council Presidency.

The deal will still need to be agreed to by the E.U. Parliament, though this process is expected to take much longer and not take place until February – this will not impact the agreement taking effect at the beginning of January.

Labour Leader Sir Keir Starmer has said that his party will back the deal when it comes to the U.K. Parliament on Wednesday (30th) because it is better than 'no deal', making it highly likely that the agreement will pass through the Commons.

30th | United Kingdom

The Oxford/AstraZeneca coronavirus vaccine has now been approved for use in the U.K. by the Medicines and Healthcare Regulatory Agency (MHRA).

It means that the U.K. now has two vaccines that it can roll out in its response to the coronavirus pandemic, with the first doses of the Oxford/AstraZeneca vaccine set to be rolled out from next week.

In a tweet, Health Secretary Matt Hancock thanked all those involved in developing the vaccine. U.K. Prime Minister Boris Johnson described the approval of the vaccine as 'truly fantastic news – and a triumph for British science'.

The U.K. has ordered around £100m doses of the vaccine, which is thought to be 62%–90% effective and can be stored at a normal fridge temperature. It is hoped that the rollout of the vaccine may be easier than the rollout of the Pfizer/BioNTech vaccine, which needs to be stored at −70°C.

On the approval of the vaccine, Professor Andrew Pollard, Director of the Oxford Vaccine Group and Chief Investigator of the Oxford Vaccine Trial, said;

> 'The regulator's assessment that this is a safe and effective
> vaccine is a landmark moment, and an endorsement of the
> huge effort from a devoted international team of researchers
> and our dedicated trial participants'.

Each U.K. nation is to receive an allocation of the vaccine based on its populations over the next weeks and months.

31st | United Kingdom

Boris Johnson's post–Brexit trade deal with the European Union has become U.K. law, after being passed by both Houses of Parliament and being granted Royal Assent.

The Brexit Deal, which was agreed between the U.K. and European Union on Christmas Eve, enters U.K. law less than a day before the end of the transition period. It means that the deal will become effective from 11pm on the 31st of December.

The House of Commons and the House of Lords were recalled during the Christmas recess in order to debate and vote on the deal. The bill was presented to MPs in the House of Commons around 9:40am on Thursday for the first time. The bill later ended the legislative process for it to become law just after midnight, following approval of the bill by the House of Lords and Her Majesty the Queen.

The bill passed comfortably through both houses, notably with a majority of 448 votes in its third and second readings in the House of Commons.

359 Conservative MPs and 162 Labour MPs voted in favour of the bill. Only 1 Labour MP voted against the bill, though 36 abstained, unhappy with the decision of their party's leader to back the deal.

When announcing the deal on the day before Christmas, U.K. Prime Minister Boris Johnson said, 'we have taken back control of our laws and our destiny'.

The new trade treaty, officially the European Union (Future Relationship) Act, will take over from the arrangements that have been in place since then under the transition period where the U.K. has had to continue to follow many E.U. rules.

31st | Worldwide

As the new year approaches, countries around the world will be celebrating it differently – not just from a normal year, but from each other.

Whilst in countries like New Zealand and Australia, the first to usher in the new year, will be celebrating almost as normal; having all but eradicated the coronavirus from their shores, other countries are forced to cancel their celebrations.

As the U.K. wishes to see the back of a year, perhaps more than at any other time in recent history, they were forced to watch new year's celebrations without the usual scale of fireworks or seeing the chiming of big ben in person.

Where many would usually be spending the new year with friends and family, attending parties or watching the fireworks, most people in the U.K. instead stayed at home. Many people were already tucked up in bed and just waiting to get 2020 over with.

'2021 will surely be better, right...?'

CONCLUSION

Despite significant scientific successes, the incredible work of heroes and extensive campaigning for positive change, 2020 will almost certainly be remembered in a negative light.

In 2020, the world tragically lost 1.8 million people to the COVID-19 Coronavirus. The direct and indirect effects of the pandemic truly changed people's lives and for many, everything and everyone lost in the year will never be forgotten.

Looking back on the year as it happened, this book has shown how the UK and other countries around the world reacted to the pandemic, which was an often fast-changing situation. Government responses varied around the world and produced both different health impacts, and public reactions.

Responses also changed over time, from closing all hospitality, to offering an entire population discounts for people to head out to their local restaurants. Balancing economic, health and a range of other pandemic impacts caused significant political debate, while lockdown breaches by public figures and lawmakers also hit the headlines.

This book has though looked at so much more than just the health emergency for which the year will mainly be remembered for. 2020 saw the rise and fall of political leadership, and the increasing advocacy of a variety of political movements. The Black Lives Matter movement called for greater racial equality, protesters tore down statues of historic slave traders and climate activists sought to advance conversations around the Climate Emergency. People came together virtually to demand an end to child food poverty, more help for struggling businesses and support for those facing the pandemic on the front line.

2020 was a year when nights in became the new nights out, online calls became the new family gatherings and daily local exercise became one of the only chances to escape the home. However physically far apart people found themselves from others in 2020, people still found ways to get through it together. Through all the challenges, 2020 showed what people can achieve when working together, from the rapid development of ground-breaking vaccines, to campaigning with others to drive positive change.

The end of 2020 was both feared, but also deeply wished for by many. Concerns over a potential no-deal scenario were dominant in the minds of many during December, though these were resolved with the agreement of a post-Brexit trade deal with the European Union just before the end of the transition period. The end of the period and the UK's departure from the single market and customs union marked the start of a new chapter in Britain's story, the contents of which is yet to be written.

The new year was welcomed in with crowds and celebrations in some parts of the world, though for many, the occasion was much more sombre, with Coronavirus continuing to require severe restrictions on civil life.

This book has covered a wide variety of important stories, focusing primarily on the U.K., with The Speaker being a U.K. media outlet, but also on stories around the world. In reality though, this book is just a snapshot of what happened in 2020.

There are a number of stories which it has not been possible to fully cover here, from elections in Myanmar, to Haitian protests. Online, The Speaker has a growing range of explainers and educational resources about political systems, institutions and key figures around the world to help the public gain a greater understanding of politics - again, explaining all of the goings on and workings of the year has not been possible in this book alone. Importantly too beyond the events which impacted wide sections of the public, everyone will have their own personal stories to tell. While it may not have provided the most opportunities, everyone who lived in 2020 will have faced new experiences which will long live on in memories, for bad or for good.

As this book goes to print, we are already two months into 2021. There is a sense of hope for a better year ahead, though tackling the Coronavirus will no doubt continue to dominant headlines. U.K. nations are back in lockdown, though with governments committing significant efforts to a rapid rollout of vaccines, there is growing hope of some return to normality in the coming weeks and months – in a year in which the U.K. will also host both the G7 Summit and an important climate summit.

In the United States, Joe Biden has entered office as the 46th U.S. President, while Kamala Harris has become the first woman in history to be sworn in as the U.S. Vice-President. Around the world, people are looking forward at both the challenges but also the hope that lies ahead.

Whatever happens in 2021 and beyond, it seems that 2020 will always have an important place in history. It will be important to look back at 2020 to consider how people got through it, what lessons can be learnt and how the world can move forward. The Speaker has always strived to educate and inspire the next generation and we hope this book helps achieve that, both in the near and more distant future.

SOURCE NOTES

This book contains adapted reporting and analysis from stories written by Nathan Shoesmith and Calum Paton, published at speakerpolitics.co.uk.

The sources noted in the section include quotes and other reports referred to in this article. In addition, this book contains some public sector information (such as but not limited to UK Coronavirus statistics) licenced under the Open Government Licence v.3.0. and Parliamentary information licenced under the Open Parliament Licence v.3.0.

International coronavirus statistics are from data aggregated by Johns Hopkins University Center for Systems Science and Engineering – see Dong Ensheng, Hongru Du, and Lauren Gardner, 'An Interactive Web-Based Dashboard to Track COVID-19 in Real Time', *The Lancet Infectious Diseases*, 20.5 (2020), 533–34 https://doi.org/10.1016/S1473-3099(20)30120-1

JANUARY

5   'At the direction of the President': Statement by the Department of
    Defense, 2 January 2020,
    https://www.defense.gov/Newsroom/Releases/Release/Article/2049534
    /statement-by-the-department-of-defense/
5   'Recognised the aggressive threat': Statement by Foreign Secretary
    Dominic Raab, 3 January 2020,
    https://www.gov.uk/government/news/iran-uk-responds-to-us-airstrike-
    on-military-commander-in-iraq
5   Reports by Politico: Trump takes massive gamble with killing of Iranian
    commander, Nahal Toosi, Daniel Lippman and Wesley Morgan for
    POLITICO, 2 January
    2020, https://www.politico.com/news/2020/01/02/soleimani-trump-
    iran-iraq-093102
5   'Vengeance is in store for the criminal': Tweet by
    @Khamenei_fa, 3 January 2020, https://twitter.com/Khamenei_fa/status
    /1212967694993100800

6 '52 Iranian targets': Tweet by @realDonaldTrump, 4 January 2020, https://twitter.com/realdonaldtrump/status/12135939746797690 93

7 'Overwhelming mandate': House of Commons Debate (Contribution by Steve Barclay), 7 January 2020, Hansard Volume 669, Column 279

8 'Absolute worst atrocities': Remarks by President Trump on Iran, 8 January 2020, https://trumpwhitehouse.archives.gov/briefings-statements/remarks-president-trump-iran/

10 'A body of information': PM (Boris Johnson) statement on Ukraine International Airlines Flight 752, 9 January 2020, https://www.gov.uk/government/speeches/pm-statement-on-ukrainian-international-airlines-flight-752

15 'An enormous expansion of the surveillance state': Big Brother Watch response to Met Police facial recognition announcement, 24 January 2020, https://bigbrotherwatch.org.uk/2020/01/big-brother-watch-response-to-met-police-facial-recognition-announcement/

15 'Move forward as one country': PM Boris Johnson signs the Withdrawal Agreement, 24 January 2020, https://www.gov.uk/government/news/pm-boris-johnson-signs-the-withdrawal-agreement-24-january-2020

17 'The main reason for this declaration': WHO Director-General's (Tedros Adhanom) statement on IHR Emergency Committee on Novel Coronavirus (2019-nCoV), 30 January 2020, https://www.who.int/director-general/speeches/detail/who-director-general-s-statement-on-ihr-emergency-committee-on-novel-coronavirus-(2019-ncov)

FEBRUARY

21 'If you're in China and able to leave, you should do so': Coronavirus and travel to China: Foreign Secretary's (Dominic Raab) statement, 4 February 2020, https://www.gov.uk/government/news/coronavirus-and-travel-to-china-foreign-secretarys-statement-4-february-2020

22 'To discuss our country's victory': Tweet by @realDonaldTrump, 5 February 2020, https://twitter.com/realdonaldtrump/status/12251790 58000089090

23 'The new cases are all known contacts': Chief Medical Officer for England announces 4 further coronavirus cases, 10 February 2020, https://www.gov.uk/government/news/chief-medical-officer-for-england-announces-four-further-coronavirus-cases

23 'Serious and imminent threat': Secretary of State makes new regulations on coronavirus, 10 February 2020 https://www.gov.uk/government/news/secretary-of-state-makes-new-regulations-on-coronavirus

24   'Today I'm launching #ComeKipWithMe': Tweet by
@RoryStewaryUK, 11 February 2020, https://twitter.com/RoryStewartUK
/status/1227165803247816705

27   'Many of you already know': Instagram Post by
@apples_symonds, 29 February 2020, https://www.instagram.com/p/B9
KMnXgAK5st_vZegXMfTrPk5BBSMRoRaJGoYY0/?igshid=pc2ex7l7b9m

28   'Been the target of a vicious and orchestrated briefing campaign': Sir
Philip Rutnam's resignation statement in full – BBC News, 29 February
2020, https://www.bbc.com/news/uk-politics-51688261,

MARCH

29   The U.K. Government has published an action plan: Coronavirus action
plan: a guide to what you can expect across the UK –
Department of Health and Social Care, 3 March 2020, https://assets.publi
shing.service.gov.uk/government/uploads/system/uploads/attachment_
data/file/869827/Coronavirus_action_plan_-
_a_guide_to_what_you_can_expect_across_the_UK.pdf

30   'I shook hands with everybody': Update on Coronavirus (COVID-19) by
Boris Johnson, 3 March 2020, Presented from Downing Street, London

31   'Penalised for doing the right thing': House of Commons Debate
(Contribution by Boris Johnson), 4 March 2020, Hansard Volume 672,
Column 827

33   'We're having an important growth in infection': Address to the Nation
by Giuseppe Conte – Televised and
broadcast live on Facebook, 9 March 2020, https://www.facebook.com/
watch/live/?v=200926397811043&ref=watch_permalink

34   'To keep new cases from entering our shores': Remarks by
President Trump in Address to the Nation, 11 March 2020, https://trump
whitehouse.archives.gov/briefings-statements/remarks-president-trump-
address-nation/

35   'Movements will be very strongly reduced': Macron announces a two-
week lockdown in France, closure of EU's Schengen zone
borders – France 24, 16 March 2020, https://www.france24.com/en/202
00316-france-s-coronavirus-situation-deteriorating-very-fast-health-
chief-says

36   Quotes from Democratic debate: Eleventh Democratic Debate,
moderated by Jake Tapper, Dana Bash and Ilia Calderón, 15 March 2020,
CNN Studio, Washington, D.C.

38   'After schools shut their gates on Friday afternoon': House of Commons
Debate (Contribution by Gavin Williamson), 18 March 2020, Hansard
Volume 673, Column 1083

38   'We can turn the tide in the next 12 weeks': Prime Minister's (Boris
Johnson) statement on coronavirus (COVID-19), 19 March 2020,

https://www.gov.uk/government/speeches/pm-statement-on-coronavirus-19-march-2020

39 'Your sacrifice means we are putting the country': Update on Coronavirus (COVID-19) by Boris Johnson, 20 March 2020, Presented from Downing Street, London

40 'We want to look back on this time and remember': Tweet by @RishiSunak, 20 March 2020, https://twitter.com/RishiSunak/status/124 1052278808883200

41 'Coronavirus is the biggest threat': Prime Minister's (Boris Johnson) statement on coronavirus (COVID-19, 23 March 2020, https://www.gov.uk/government/speeches/pm-address-to-the-nation-on-coronavirus-23-march-2020

42 'We are seeking a quarter of a million volunteers': Update on Coronavirus (COVID-19) by Matt Hancock, 24 March 2020, Presented from Downing Street, London

43 'Over the last 24 hours I have developed mild symptoms': Tweet by @BorisJohnson, 27 March 2020, https://twitter.com/BorisJohnson/status/1243496858095411200

APRIL

45 'It is the honour and privilege of my life': Video Tweet by @UKLabour, 4 April 2020, https://twitter.com/UKLabour/status/1246385 962818637825

47 'While we have faced challenges before': The Queen's broadcast to the UK and Commonwealth – BBC Studios Events, 5 April 2020, https://www.youtube.com/watch?v=bP_hNq6-0S8

48 'Confident' that Prime Minister Boris Johnson will 'pull–through': Foreign Secretary's statement on coronavirus (COVID-19), 7 April 2020, https://www.gov.uk/government/speeches/foreign-secretarys-statement-on-coronavirus-covid-19-7-april-2020

48 'We'll see if we can be of help': Remarks by President Trump in Press Briefing, 6 April 2020, https://trumpwhitehouse.archives.gov/briefings-statements/remarks-president-trump-vice-president-pence-members-coronavirus-task-force-press-briefing-21/

49 'A speedy recovery': Tweet by @Keir_Starmer, 9 April 2020, https://twitter.com/Keir_Starmer/status/1248322348832391171

50 'It's hard to find the words to express my debt': Tweet by @BorisJohnson, 12 April 2020, https://twitter.com/Keir_Starmer/status/1248322348832391171

50 'The biggest meltdown from a U.S. President': Jim Acosta speaking on OutFront, CNN, 14 April 2020

50 'We've done this right': Press Briefing by Donald Trump, 14 April 2020, Presented from The White House, Washington D.C.

51   The International Monetary Fund (IMF) has released a report: World
       Economic Outlook, April 2020: The Great Lockdown –
       International Monetary Fund, 14 April 2020, https://www.imf.org/en/Pu
       blications/WEO/Issues/2020/04/14/weo-april-2020

51   'Thank you so much to everyone': Tweet by @captaintommoore,
       16 April 2020, https://twitter.com/captaintommoore/status/1250699933
       268807680

52   'Completely out of this world': Coronavirus: Captain Tom Moore raises
       more than £9m for NHS – BBC News, 15 April 2020,
       https://www.bbc.com/news/uk-england-beds-bucks-herts-52290976

53   'A crucial five weeks in the fight to tackle the dangerous threat':
       Coronavirus: 38 days when Britain sleepwalked into disaster by Jonathan
       Calvert, George Arbuthnott and Jonathan Leake for The
       Sunday Times, 19 April 2020, https://www.thetimes.co.uk/article/corona
       virus-38-days-when-britain-sleepwalked-into-disaster-hq3b9tlgh

53   'The idea that the Prime Minister skipped meetings': Sky News Sophy
       Ridge on Sunday – Interview with Michael Gove, 19 April 2020

53   'Most COBRA meetings don't have the Prime Minister': BBC Andrew Marr
       Show – Interview with Michael Gove, 19 April 2020

53   'Rigorously scientific': Dogs could join the fight against COVID-19
       – Medical Detection Dogs, 27 March 2020, https://www.medicaldetectio
       ndogs.org.uk/dogs-could-join-the-fight-against-covid-19/

54   UV lights in order to 'kill it': Remarks by President Trump in Press
       Briefing, 23 April 2020, https://trumpwhitehouse.archives.gov/briefings-
       statements/remarks-president-trump-vice-president-pence-members-
       coronavirus-task-force-press-briefing-31/

55   'Biological sex based on primary sex characteristics': Draft Bill Submission
       - On the Amendment of Certain Administrative Laws and on the Free
       Transfer of Property (quote
       from pg.10, translated), 31 March 2020, https://www.parlament.hu/irom
       41/09934/09934.pdf

57   'So thrilled for Boris and Carrie': Tweet by @MattHancock, 29
       April 2020, https://twitter.com/MattHancock/status/1255422449119879
       171

57   'Wonderful news. Many congratulations': Tweet by
       @Keir_Starmer, 29 April 2020, https://twitter.com/Keir_Starmer/status/
       1255422995335712781

57   'Past the peak and on the downward slope': Prime Minister's statement
       on coronavirus (COVID-19), 30 April 2020,
       https://www.gov.uk/government/news/prime-ministers-statement-on-
       coronavirus-covid-19-30-april-2020

58   'The tests I did for coronavirus came back positive': Mikhail Mishustin
       during televised video meeting with Vladimir Putin on 30 April 2020

MAY

64   The United Kingdom faces a 'significant recession': Channel 4 News interview with Chancellor Rishi Sunak, 13 May 2020, https://www.channel4.com/news/it-is-now-very-likely-that-the-uk-economy-is-facing-a-significant-recession-chancellor-rishi-sunak

64   Economy has shrunk by 2% over the first quarter: GDP monthly estimate, UK - Office for National Statistics – by James Scuton, 13 May 2020, https://www.ons.gov.uk/economy/grossdomesticproductgdp/bulletins/gdpmonthlyestimateuk/march2020

65   The jobs 'are gone for good': Tweet by @AndrewYang, 15 May 2020, https://twitter.com/andrewyang/status/1261085055839076358

66   'Novel and unbalanced proposals': David Frost's statement at the end of round 3 negotiations with the EU - No 10 media blog, 15 May 2020, https://no10media.blog.gov.uk/2020/05/15/david-frosts-statement-at-the-end-of-round-3-negotiations-with-the-eu/

68   'I am absolutely overwhelmed': Tweet by @captaintommoore, 20 May 2020, https://twitter.com/captaintommoore/status/1263008988523888641

69   'I know how ill coronavirus makes you': Tweet by @MattHancock, 23 May 2020, https://twitter.com/MattHancock/status/1264162359733555202

69   Reopening schools would be 'tough': Prime Minister's (Boris Johnson) statement on coronavirus (COVID-19), 24 May 2020, https://www.gov.uk/government/speeches/pm-press-conference-statement-24-may-2020

70   Nicola Sturgeon has tweeted a reminder: Tweet by @NicolaSturgeon, 24 May 2020, https://twitter.com/NicolaSturgeon/status/1264591700267356160

70   Cabinet Office later announced it was investigating the matter: Tweet by @cabinetofficeuk, 24 May 2020, https://twitter.com/cabinetofficeuk/status/1264613950790008835

70   Believed he was acting 'reasonably': Press Briefing delivered by Dominic Cummings, 25 May 2020, Presented from Downing Street, London

74   Measures are 'cautious': Prime Minister's statement on coronavirus (COVID-19), 28 May 2020, https://www.gov.uk/government/speeches/pm-press-conference-statement-on-the-five-tests-28-may-2020

74   Terminating its relationship: Press Briefing from the Rose Garden by President Trump, 29 May 2020, Presented from The White House, Washington D.C.

75   'CHINA!': Tweet by @realDonaldTrump, 29 May 2020, https://twitter.com/realdonaldtrump/status/1266354084036194306

75   Ms Duffield met her partner for a five-hour walk: Labour MP Rosie Duffield stands down as whip after breaking coronavirus lockdown rules

– by Scarlet Howes and Brendan Carlin for Mail on Sunday, 31 May 2020, https://www.dailymail.co.uk/news/article-8373103/Labour-MP-Rosie-Duffield-stands-whip-breaking-coronavirus-lockdown-rules.html

JUNE

77   'Dominate the streets': Statement by the President (Donald Trump), 1 June 2020, https://trumpwhitehouse.archives.gov/briefings-statements/statement-by-the-president-39/

78   End the 'virtual commons': Proceedings during the Pandemic (Division 52) – Hansard, 2 June 2020, https://hansard.parliament.uk/Commons/2020-06-02/division/A2B464BD-B136-4502-A0DB-3ED92E728AAD/ProceedingsDuringThePandemicoutputType=Names

79   The wearing of face masks on public transport: Transport Secretary's statement on coronavirus (COVID-19), 4 June 2020, https://www.gov.uk/government/speeches/transport-secretarys-statement-on-coronavirus-covid-19-4-june-2020

80   'Like so many, I am appalled': Health and Social Care Secretary's statement on coronavirus (COVID-19), 5 June 2020, https://www.gov.uk/government/speeches/health-and-social-care-secretarys-statement-on-coronavirus-covid-19-5-june-2020

80   'Utterly disgraceful': Priti Patel: Toppling Edward Colston statue 'utterly disgraceful' – Sky News, 7 June 2020, https://news.sky.com/video/priti-patel-toppling-edward-colston-statue-utterly-disgraceful-12002452

81   All five tests for easing lockdown measures are being met: Prime Minister's (Boris Johnson) statement on coronavirus (COVID-19), 10 June 2020, https://www.gov.uk/government/speeches/pm-statement-at-the-coronavirus-press-conference-10-june-2020

82   'Diminishes Britain's place in the world': Tweet by @Keir_Starmer, 16 June 2020, https://twitter.com/keir_starmer/status/1272918142533107713?lang=en

83   'All persons held as slaves': Transcript of the Proclamation – January 1, 1863, Published online on 6 October 2015, https://www.archives.gov/exhibits/featured-documents/emancipation-proclamation/transcript.html

85   Article she had shared on Twitter: Maxine Peake: 'People who couldn't vote Labour because of Jeremy Corbyn? They voted Tory as far as I'm concerned' – The Independent, 25 June 2020, https://www.independent.co.uk/arts-entertainment/films/features/maxine-peake-interview-labour-corbyn-keir-starmer-black-lives-matter-a9583206.html

85   'In no way was my retweet an intention to endorse': Tweet by @RLong_Bailey, 25 June 2020, https://twitter.com/RLong_Bailey/status/1276161742104678407

191

86   Six people are being treated in hospital: Latest information on West
George Street incident, Glasgow - Police Scotland, 26 June 2020,
https://www.scotland.police.uk/what-s-happening/news/2020/june/late
st-information-on-west-george-street-incident-glasgow/

87   Prosecutor, Ali Alqasimehr, announced the charges: Iran issues arrest
warrant for Trump; Interpol denies help – Al Jazeera, 30 June 2020,
ehttps://www.aljazeera.com/news/2020/6/30/iran-issues-arrest-
warrant-for-trump-interpol-denies-help

87   'It sounds positively Rooseveltian': Prime Minister announces
New Deal for Britain – Press Release, 30 June 2020, https://www.gov.uk/
government/news/build-build-build-prime-minister-announces-new-
deal-for-britain

JULY

90   'Its criminal provisions are worded': Legislation Summary: Hong Kong
National Security Law - by NPC Observer, 30 June 2020, https://npcobser
ver.com/2020/06/30/legislation-summary-hong-kong-national-security-
law/

92   'Little flu': Televised Interview with R7 (Statement by Jair Bolsonaro), 22
March 2020

92   'People need to know': House of Commons Debate (Statement by Rishi
Sunak), 8 July 2020, Hansard Volume 678, Column 973

94   'Improper Request': Statement by Julian Lewis MP, 15 July 2020,
Statement to PA News Agency

95   'Immediately and indefinitely': House of Commons Debate (Statement by
Dominic Raab), 20 July 2020, Hansard Volume 678, Column 1832

97   'One of Russia's top': Russia Report (House of Commons Intelligence and
Security Committee), 21 July 2020 https://isc.independent.gov.uk/news-
archive/21july2020

98   Various alleged interactions: Delyn MP Rob Roberts Invited Intern to
'Fool Around' with Him – by Ione Wells and Katrin Haf Jones for BBC
News, 21 July 2020, www.bbc.co.uk/news/uk-wales-politics-53472289.

AUGUST

103   'Bigger than the state': Resignation Speech by Hassan Diab, 10 August
2020, https://english.alarabiya.net/features/2020/08/10/Read-full-
resignation-speech-of-Lebanese-PM-Hassan-Diab

104   'The violence and the attempts': UK Statement: Belarussian Presidential
Elections 2020 (James Duddridge), 10 August 2020, https://www.gov.uk/
government/news/uk-statement-belarusian-presidential-elections-2020

104   'I know that it works': Televised Statement by Russian President on
coronavirus vaccine (Statement by Vladimir Putin), 11 August 2020,

https://www.cbsnews.com/news/covid-vaccine-russia-coronavirus-development/

107 'We recognise that': Statement by Roger Taylor, Chair of Ofqual, 17 August 2020, https://www.gov.uk/government/news/statement-from-roger-taylor-chair-ofqual

109 'Seems unlikely': Remarks by Michel Barnier, 21 August https://ec.europa.eu/commission/presscorner/detail/en/statement_20_1511

109 'Still possible and it is still our goal': David Frost's statement following the conclusion of round 7 negotiations with the EU, 21 August 2020, https://no10media.blog.gov.uk/2020/08/21/david-frosts-statement-following-the-conclusion-of-round-7-negotiations-with-the-eu/

109 'Considerable gaps remain': David Frost's statement following the conclusion of round 5 negotiations with the EU, 23 July 2020, https://no10media.blog.gov.uk/2020/07/23/david-frosts-statement-following-the-conclusion-of-round-5-negotiations-with-the-eu/

110 'It is important to build on': Foreign Secretary to press for renewed dialogue in Israel and OPTs (Dominic Raab), 24 August 2020, https://www.gov.uk/government /news/foreign-sec-to-press-for-renewed-dialogue-in-israel-and-opts

111 'National listening project': It is time for us to start listening (Statement by Sir Edward Davey), 27 August 2020, https://www.libdems.org.uk/ed-davey-new-leader-speech

111 'I look forward to working with him': Tweet by @LaylaMoran, 27 August 2020, https://twitter.com/LaylaMoran/status/1298937087337680896

SEPTEMBER

115 'Unifying step': FareShare joins child poverty task force spearheaded by England International footballer Marcus Rashford, 1 September 2020, https://fareshare.org.uk/news-media/press-releases/fareshare-joins-child-poverty-task-force-spearheaded-by-england-international-footballer-marcus-rashford/

116 'If he wants to know what misogyny looks like': Australian House of Representatives debate (Statement by Julia Gillard), 10 October 2012, https://www.smh.com.au/politics/federal/transcript-of-julia-gillards-speech-20121010-27c36.html

117 'If holding misogynistic, homophobic, Trump-backing': Controversial figure Tony Abbott given Board of Trade adviser role – by Hannah Carmichael for The National (quote from Kirsten Oswald), 4 September 2020, https://www.thenational.scot/news/18699300.controversial-figure-tony-abbott-given-board-trade-adviser-role/

117 'Seamless functioning': Bill introduced to protect jobs and trade across the whole of the United Kingdom – press release, 8 September 2020,

https://www.gov.uk/government/news/bill-introduced-to-protect-jobs-and-trade-across-the-whole-of-the-united-kingdom

119   'Protect Trade and Jobs': Bill introduced to protect jobs and trade across the whole of the United Kingdom – press release, 8 September 2020, https://www.gov.uk/government/news/bill-introduced-to-protect-jobs-and-trade-across-the-whole-of-the-united-kingdom

120   'Any other provision or rule': United Kingdom Internal Market Bill (as introduced), 9 September 2020, https://publications.parliament.uk/pa/bills/cbill/58-01/0177/20177.pdf

120   'Very specific and limited way': House of Commons Debate (Statement by Brandon Lewis), 14 September 2020, Hansard Volume 680, Column 509

120   'What incompetence': House of Commons Debate (Contribution by Ed Miliband), 14 September 2020, Hansard Volume 680, Column 52.

122   Academics Clive Hamilton and Mareike Ohlberg in their book: Clive Hamilton, and Mareike Ohlberg. HIDDEN HAND: Exposing How the Chinese Communist Party Is Reshaping the World. S.L., Oneworld Publications, 2021.

123   'Never articulated the national security rationale': TikTok to Be Banned from US App Stores from Sunday – by Demetri Sevastopulo and James Fontanella-Khan for Financial Times (quote from Demetri Sevastopulo), 18 Sept. 2020, www.ft.com/content/c460ce4c-c691-4df5-af49-47a395429fe8

123   'I struck out on three grounds': The Three Lessons You Can Learn From Ruth Bader Ginsburg About Ambition – Bonnie Marcus for Forbes (quote from Ruth Bader Ginsburg), quote published widely, including by Forbes on 12 November 2018, https://www.forbes.com/sites/bonniemarcus/2018/11/12/the-three-lessons-you-can-learn-from-ruth-bader-ginsburg-about-ambition/?sh=2b38522d17d9

124   'Fight for the things that you care about': Ruth Bader Ginsburg Tells Young Women: 'Fight For The Things You Care About' – Harvard Radcliffe Institute, published on 6 February 2015, https://www.radcliffe.harvard.edu/news-and-ideas/ruth-bader-ginsburg-tells-young-women-fight-for-the-things-you-care-about

124   'Women belong in all places': Justice Ginsburg ready to welcome Sotomayor - by Bill Mears for CNN, 16 June 2009, https://edition.cnn.com/2009/POLITICS/06/16/sotomayor.ginsburg/index.html

124   'Real change, enduring change': Notorious RBG: The Life and Times of Ruth Bader Ginsburg – by Irin Cameron (2015), Dey Street Books (quote from Ruth Bader Ginsburg)

125   '50,000 cases per day by mid–October': Chief Medical Officer's statement on coronavirus (COVID-19), 21st September 2020, https://www.gov.uk/government/speeches/chief-scientific-advisor-and-chief-medical-officer-briefing-on-coronavirus-covid-19-21-september-2020--2

128 'Never again': Full text of Keir Starmer's speech at Labour Connected, 22 September 2020, https://labour.org.uk/press/full-text-of-keir-starmers-speech-at-labour-connected/

129 According to a New York Times exposé: Trump's Taxes Show Chronic Losses and Years of Income Tax Avoidance – by Russ Buettner, Susanne Craig and Mike McIntire for The New York Times, 27 September 2020, www.nytimes.com/interactive/2020/09/27/us/donald-trump-taxes.html

130 'Clearly this debate was an embarrassment for the United States': Transcript by CNN (transcription of Wolf Blitzer, CNN Host), transcripts.cnn.com/TRANSCRIPTS/2009/29/se.05.html

OCTOBER

133 'This draft bill is': Press statement by President von der Leyen on the implementation of the Withdrawal Agreement between the EU and the UK, 1 October 2020, https://ec.europa.eu/commission/presscorner/detail/en/statement_20_1800

134 'Tonight, @FLOTUS and I': Tweet by @realDonaldTrump, 2 October 2020, https://twitter.com/realdonaldtrump/status/1311892190680014849

134 'Best wishes to President Trump': Tweet by @BorisJohnson, 2 October 2020, https://twitter.com/BorisJohnson/status/1311938117872619520

135 'Praying for their full and swift recovery': Tweet by @Mike_Pence, 2 October 2020, https://twitter.com/Mike_Pence/status/1311908650269765638

135 'Don't be afraid of COVID': Tweet by @realDonaldTrump, 5 October 2020,https://twitter.com/realdonaldtrump/status/1313186529058136070

136 'Build Back Better': Boris Johnson: Read the Prime Minister's Keynote Speech in Full, 6 October 2020, www.conservatives.com/news/boris-johnson-read-the-prime-ministers-keynote-speech-in-full

138 'You must not meet socially with friends and family': Statement by Health Secretary Matt Hancock, 15 October 2020, https://www.gov.uk/government/speeches/coronavirus-update-on-areas-in-local-covid-alert-levels

138 'Situation in Greater Manchester is grave': Prime Minister's (Boris Johnson) statement on coronavirus (COVID-19), https://www.gov.uk/government/speeches/prime-ministers-statement-on-coronavirus-covid-19-16-october-2020

139 'New Zealand has shown the Labour Party its greatest support': Statement by Jacinda Ardern, 17 October 2020, https://www.rev.com/blog/transcripts/new-zealand-pm-jacinda-ardern-victory-speech-transcript-wins-2020-new-zealand-election

141 'If we pull hard together over the next six weeks': Statement of An Taoiseach Micheál Martin announcing Ireland moving to Level 5, 19

October 2020, https://www.gov.ie/en/speech/f122e-statement-of-an-taoiseach-micheal-martin-announcing-ireland-moving-to-level-5/

143 'A Polish sexual and reproductive health and rights activist, who spoke to the BBC': Poland Abortion: Top Court Bans Almost All Terminations by BBC News (quote from Antonina Lewandowska, 23 October 2020, www.bbc.co.uk/news/world-europe-54642108

145 'My most feverent wish': Ginsburg's Wish: 'I Will Not Be Replaced until a New President Is Installed' by Matthew Choi and Josh Gerstein for POLITICO (quote dictated to Clara Spera and published by POLITCO), 18 September 2020 www.politico.com/news/2020/09/18/ginsburg-rbg-dying-wish-418108

146 'I am grateful to the EHRC for its comprehensive investigation' Blog post by @lucianaberger on Medium, 29 October 2020, medium.com/@lucian aberger_76642/i-am-grateful-to-the-ehrc-for-its-comprehensive-investigation-which-today-finds-the-the-labour-43391203d62e

146 'If – after all the pain': Statement by Keir Starmer, 29 October 2020, https://labour.org.uk/press/keir-starmers-statement-in-response-to-ehrcs-report-into-anti-semitism/

NOVEMBER

154 'Fake polls': Remarks by President Trump on the Election, 5 November 2020, https://trumpwhitehouse.archives.gov/briefings-statements/remarks-president-trump-election/

157 'Great day for science and humanity': Pfizer and BioNTech Announce Vaccine Candidate Against COVID-19 Achieved Success in First Interim Analysis from Phase 3 Study, 9 November 2020, https://www.pfizer.com/news/press-release/press-release-detail/pfizer-and-biontech-announce-vaccine-candidate-against

159 'This campaign to harass, stifle and disqualify democratic opposition': Foreign Secretary statement on the expulsion of pro-democracy legislators in Hong Kong, 11 November 2020, https://www.gov.uk/government/news/foreign-secretary-statement-on-the-expulsion-of-pro-democracy-legislators-in-hong-kong

160 'The time has come in the interest of the country': Tweet by @SirRogerGale, 12 November 2020, https://twitter.com/SirRogerGale/status/1326889030466854914

161 'Jeremy Corbyn's actions in response to the EHRC report': Tweet by @Keir_Starmer, 18 November 2020, https://twitter.com/Keir_Starmer/status/1329017097385615362

163 'I feel that it is right that I should now resign': Statement from Sir Alex Allan, 20 November 2020, https://www.gov.uk/government/news/statement-from-sir-alex-allan

163 Back closer to normality by Christmas: Prime Minister's statement on coronavirus (COVID-19), 17 July 2020,

https://www.gov.uk/government/speeches/pm-statement-on-coronavirus-17-july-2020

164   Moderna vaccine 95% effective: Moderna's COVID-19 Vaccine Candidate Meets its Primary Efficacy Endpoint in the First Interim Analysis of the Phase 3 COVE Study, 16 November 2020, https://investors.modernatx.com/news-releases/news-release-details/modernas-covid-19-vaccine-candidate-meets-its-primary-efficacy

164   'The ChAdOx1 nCov–2019 coronavirus vaccine': Oxford coronavirus vaccine produces strong immune response in older adults, 19 November 2020, https://www.ox.ac.uk/news/2020-11-19-oxford-coronavirus-vaccine-produces-strong-immune-response-older-adults

165   'I believe it is fundamentally wrong': Image Tweet by @liz_sugg, 25 November 2020, https://twitter.com/liz_sugg/status/1331619532687945730

166   'Difficult to justify': House of Commons Debate (Contribution by Rishi Sunak), 25 November 2020, Hansard Volume 684, Column 830

DECEMBER

169   'This is a momentous occasion': COVID-19 vaccine authorised by medicines regulator, 2 December 2020, https://www.gov.uk/government/news/covid-19-vaccine-authorised-by-medicines-regulator

169   'Today we are taking the lead': UK sets ambitious new climate target ahead of UN Summit (quote from Boris Johnson, 3 December 2020, https://www.gov.uk/government/news/uk-sets-ambitious-new-climate-target-ahead-of-un-summit

169   In a statement released by Merseyside Police: Five arrested as part of fraud investigation, 4 December 2020, https://www.merseyside.police.uk/news/merseyside/news/2020/december/five-people-arrested-as-part-of-fraud-investigation/

170   'As agreed on Saturday': Joint Statement from UK Prime Minister Boris Johnson and European Commission President von der Leyen, 7 December 2020, https://www.gov.uk/government/news/joint-statement-from-uk-prime-minister-boris-johnson-and-european-commission-president-von-der-leyen-7-december-2020

170   'So proud to be British': Good Morning Britain, interview with Health Secretary Matt Hancock, 8 December 2020

171   'I look forward to welcoming': Tweet by @vonderleyen, 8 December 2020, https://twitter.com/vonderleyen/status/1336366191930187779

171   'We are taking action to stand up for the millions': Tweet by @NewYorkStateAG, 9 December 2020, https://twitter.com/NewYorkStateAG/status/1336755231946846208

172   'We look forward to our day in court': Lawsuits Filed by the FTC and the State Attorneys General Are Revisionist History – by

Jennifer Newstead for Facebook, 9 December 2020, https://about.fb.com
/news/2020/12/lawsuits-filed-by-the-ftc-and-state-attorneys-general-
are-revisionist-history/

173   'Unanimous Agreement': House of Commons Debate (Contribution by
      Boris Johnson), 16 December 2020, Hansard Volume 686, Column 266

173   'We believe the government is about to blunder': Covid 19: Christmas
      relaxation will overwhelm services, 15 December 2020,
      https://www.bmj.com/content/371/bmj.m4847

174   'We cannot continue with Christmas as planned': Update on Coronavirus
      (COVID-19) by Boris Johnson, 19 December 2020, Presented from
      Downing Street, London

176   'Sadly, the measures the government announced yesterday': Online
      Press Conference by Sir Keir Starmer, 20 December 2020

177   'Had a very good call': Prime Minister's statement on coronavirus
      (COVID-19), 21 December 2020, https://www.gov.uk/government/speec
      hes/prime-ministers-statement-on-coronavirus-covid-19-21-december-
      2020

179   'The regulator's assessment that this is a safe and effective vaccine':
      AstraZeneca's COVID-19 vaccine authorised for emergency supply in the
      UK (quote from Professor Andrew
      Pollard), 30 December 2020, https://www.astrazeneca.com/media-
      centre/press-releases/2020/astrazenecas-covid-19-vaccine-authorised-
      in-uk.html

180   'We have taken back control of our laws and destiny': Prime Minister's
      statement on EU negotiations, 24 December 2020,
      https://www.gov.uk/government/speeches/prime-ministers-statement-
      on-eu-negotiations-24-december-2020

ACKNOWLEDGEMENTS

It is more typical for acknowledgements to focus on the people that have helped on the journey to creating this book. To that end, we wish to thank the army of family, friends and academic colleagues who have assisted in proof reading and inspiring the development of our first foray into print.

However, it is perhaps more appropriate to acknowledge the people that have made The Speaker possible. The Speaker started with a simple but important mission: to inspire the next generation in politics. Developing The Speaker into what it is today has been enjoyable; however, it has taken time and perservance. While we are directors of The Speaker, we are not the only people who have put their time and support into it and ultimately recognised the importance of the mission. While there are too many to name here, we extend our thanks to everyone who has been part of the journey to date and that has offered their continuous support.

We want to thank our family and friends – those interested and uninterested in politics. Without your support and heartfelt friendship, our work to date would not have been possible. Quite often when around you, our minds may be partially elsewhere – thinking about the important questions to pose on press conferences or considering the most important stories to highlight in this book. Thank you for putting up with us and for all you that you do.

It was at times an arduous experience for those assisting as proof-readers or sounding boards for this book – we'd like to thank each one of you. Calum would particularly like to thank Bette King and Bethany Burns for their help in diligently proofreading, taking this book from its first draft to now.

We should also offer our sincere gratitude to a number of educational professionals that have believed in us, offered us opportunities and inspiration and have long supported The Speaker through its development; in particular, Nathan would like to mention Chris Smith and Richard Baguley.

We, in our acknowledgements, as in our coverage, will not have been able to cover everyone and everything worthy of acknowledgement. To any that we have not been acknowledged directly here, just know that your support is invaluable and greatly appreciated.

Calum and Nathan.

ABOUT THE SPEAKER

The Speaker is an impartial news media company on a mission to inspire the next generation in politics.

Setup in Norwich, U.K., in 2018, The Speaker was founded by a group of students who felt that there wasn't really anything out there making politics accessible and understandable for the wider public, but particularly for young people. Starting as an idea in the classroom, The Speaker has grown massively over recent years and become a trusted source of political coverage.

Today, The Speaker reaches audiences throughout the U.K. and around the world through its impartial and explanatory coverage of top political news stories. In times of wide scale political change, it has never been more important that young people can understand politics, get involved and have their say. Through its Education Service, The Speaker helps increase young peoples' understanding and engagement in politics, while saving teachers and educational leaders time.

Stories in this book are adapted from The Speaker's coverage of events in 2020, as reported by Nathan Shoesmith and Calum Paton.

TO LEARN MORE ABOUT THE SPEAKER, VISIT SPEAKERPOLITICS.CO.UK.

ABOUT THE AUTHORS

CALUM PATON

Calum is the Deputy Managing Director of The Speaker, having joined the company just months after it was founded. He is currently studying for a masters in law, having graduated from the University of Warwick in 2020, with a degree in history and politics.

Having started writing about politics almost a decade ago, Calum has won several student journalism awards and has written for media outlets in multiple countries. When joining The Speaker in 2018, Calum operated out of Melbourne, Australia, acting as the global news manager, before becoming deputy managing director and later a company director, during a period that has seen The Speaker grow to become the outlet it is today.

Calum has been involved in a number of charitable projects, including a campaign to raise awareness of domestic violence in teenage relationships, as well as taking part in regular pro bono projects whilst studying for his masters.

CALUM@SPEAKERPOLITICS.CO.UK

NATHAN SHOESMITH

Nathan is the Managing Director and one of the co–founders of The Speaker, currently studying Management, Politics & International Relations at Lancaster University in the north-west of England.

From a young age, Nathan has been committed to supporting others, from creating opportunities through sports coaching and charitable work, to increasing access to understandable knowledge through roles in media. In 2019, Nathan was recognised as an 'inspirational young leader' and featured in The Independent's Happy List - a list 'celebrating 50 of the most inspirational people whose kindness, ingenuity and bravery have made Britain a better place to live'.

Nathan has taken part in a number of campaigns to raise awareness of important issues. In recent years, Nathan has been keen to raise awareness of mental health charities, recognising the importance of removing the stigma around mental health. In particular, during 2020, many people experienced mental health problems for the first time as a result of Coronavirus lockdown measures and Nathan himself faced a period of struggles following a head injury. Since 2014, Nathan has led a range of campaigns that have raised awareness and over £10,000 for a range of important charitable causes.

A big fan of sport and travelling, Nathan can often be found exploring new places, watching and playing sport in non-lockdown times.

NATHAN@SPEAKERPOLITICS.CO.UK